THE CONCISE GUIDE TO

JUDAISM

HISTORY, PRACTICE, FAITH

THE CONCISE GUIDE TO
JUDAISM
HISTORY, PRACTICE, FAITH

Roy A. Rosenberg

NAL BOOKS

NAL BOOKS
Published by the Penguin Group
Penguin Books USA Inc., 375 Hudson Street,
New York, New York 10014, U.S.A.
Penguin Books Ltd, 27 Wrights Lane,
London W8 5TZ, England
Penguin Books Australia Ltd, Ringwood,
Victoria, Australia
Penguin Books Canada Ltd, 2801 John Street,
Markham, Ontario, Canada L3R 1B4
Penguin Books (N.Z.) Ltd, 182-190 Wairau Road,
Auckland 10, New Zealand

Penguin Books Ltd, Registered Offices:
Harmondsworth, Middlesex, England

First published by NAL Books, an imprint of Penguin Books USA Inc.
Published simultaneously in Canada.

First Printing, May, 1990
10 9 8 7 6 5 4 3 2 1

 REGISTERED TRADEMARK—MARCA REGISTRADA

Library of Congress Cataloging-in-Publication Data

Rosenberg, Roy A., 1930–
    The concise guide to Judaism : history, practice, faith / Roy A. Rosenberg.
        p.   cm.
    ISBN 0-453-00728-7
    1. Judaism. I. Title.
BM561.R62 1990
296—dc20   89-13616
                                                            CIP

PRINTED IN THE UNITED STATES OF AMERICA
Set in Times Roman
Designed by Leonard Telesca

To My Teachers

Psalm 119:99 reads, "Beyond all my teachers have I gained wisdom, for Your testimonies are conversation to me." The rabbis, however, read the text to mean, "From all my teachers have I gained wisdom." Presumably, I have learned more than some of my teachers; others, however, are wiser than I will ever be. From all of them have I learned, and to all of them I dedicate this book. Some of them I have known personally; others I know only from the written word. Some have been devoted to Judaism as an immutable system of law and doctrine; others have sought to reshape the teachings of the faith so that its essence can continue to inform human hearts even as its outward forms change. Some have gone through fire and water for the sake of their faith, suffering even unto death. Others have lived lives of serenity and contentment. The work of all of them lives on, in me and in others who have learned from them. Their work gives life to the Jewish people and its faith. Their work is the work of God, for they transmit His Teaching to men and women who, though but flesh and blood, yet share in His Image.

Contents

Acknowledgments

It is customary for authors to thank their editors, but in the case of Alexia Dorszynski much more than a formal word is in order. Her intelligence and sense of style have contributed much to the manuscript, and she suggested several of the topics I have sought to cover. If the book should be of value to students and general readers, which has been our hope and desire, much of the credit belongs to her. She has also been a pleasure to work with, for which I am most grateful. If this book succeeds in informing its readers about Judaism in its various aspects, readers should be grateful to her too.

A number of people read portions of the manuscript and made good suggestions. I am particularly grateful to three people, however, who read the manuscript in its entirety: Rabbi A. Stanley Dreyfus, Ph.D.; Rabbi Etan Levine, Ph.D.; and Rabbi Maurice Portnoy, Ph.D., who were ordained, respectively, by the faculties of the Hebrew Union College, the Jewish Theological Seminary of America, and the Rabbi Isaac Elchanan Theological Seminary. All of them made a number of important suggestions that I incorporated into the manuscript's final version. As might be expected, however, I did not accept all of the recommendations that they made, so none of them should be held responsible in the least degree for any inadequacies or misconceptions that the book is heir to. Any errors or misrepresentations are solely my own, and I hereby apologize for them in advance. As the Bible teaches, it is only God's work that is perfect (Deuteronomy 32:4).

—Roy A. Rosenberg

September 29, 1989
Eve of Rosh haShana, 5750
New York, N. Y.

Listed below are the works that have been quoted in the book.

Biblical citations have been compared with *The Holy Bible: Revised Standard Version*, New York: Thomas Nelson, 1952.

Citations from the Mishna have been compared with the translation by Herbert Danby, *The Mishnah*, London: Oxford University Press, 1933.

Citations from the Babylonian Talmud have been compared with the translation of the Soncino Press, London, 1935–1948.

The responsum of Rabbenu Hananel of Kairwan was translated by Jacob Z. Lauterbach, *The Jewish Encyclopedia*, vol. 11, p. 245, New York: Funk and Wagnalls Co., 1905.

The selection from Philo was translated from the Greek by F. H. Colson and G. H. Whitaker, *Loeb Classical Library: Philo*, Cambridge: Harvard University Press, 1962.

The selection from Saadia was translated from the Arabic by Samuel Rosenblatt, *The Book of Beliefs and Opinions*, New Haven: Yale University Press, 1948.

The selection from Judah haLevi was translated from the Arabic by Hartwig Hirschfeld, *Judah Hallevi's Kitab al Khazari*, London: M. L. Cailingold, 1931.

The selection from Zohar II, 113b, was translated by Harry Sperling, Maurice Simon, and Paul P. Levertoff, *The Zohar*, London: Soncino Press, 1933.

The discussion of the Lurianic kabbala was taken from Gershom Scholem, "The Doctrine of Creation in Lurianic Kabbalah," *Kabbalah*, New York: Quadrangle, 1974.

The selection from Moses Mendelssohn was translated from the German by Isaac Leeser, *Jerusalem*, Philadelphia: G. Sherman, 1852.

The selection from Franz Rosenzweig was translated from the German by William W. Hallo, *The Star of Redemption*, New York: Holt, Rinehart and Winston, 1971.

The selection from Martin Buber comes from *The Philosophy of Martin Buber*, edited by Paul Arthur Schilpp and Maurice Friedman, La Salle, IL: Open Court Publishing Co., 1967.

The discussion of Abraham Joshua Heschel was taken in part from an unpublished lecture by Dr. Ruth Rosenberg. The selection from Heschel is from *God in Search of Man*, New York: Farrar, Straus and Cudahy, 1955.

The selection from Mordecai Kaplan comes from *Judaism as a Civilization*, New York: Macmillan Publishing Co., 1934.

The translation of the *unetaneh tokef* prayer is by Arthur Davis. It was first published in England, and reprinted in New Year and Atonement prayerbooks published by the Hebrew Publishing Co., New York (no date given).

Translations of other texts are by the author.

THE CONCISE GUIDE TO
JUDAISM
HISTORY, PRACTICE, FAITH

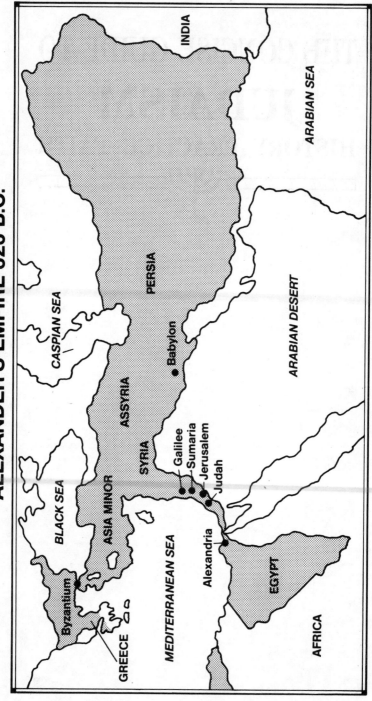

ALEXANDER'S EMPIRE 323 B.C.

INDIA

ARABIAN SEA

CASPIAN SEA

PERSIA

Babylon

ASSYRIA

ARABIAN DESERT

BLACK SEA

SYRIA

ASIA MINOR

Galilee
Sumaria
Jerusalem
Judah

Byzantium

MEDITERRANEAN SEA

Alexandria

GREECE

EGYPT

AFRICA

CHAPTER ONE

"A People That Dwells Alone"

Over the ages people have wondered, "Why did God choose the Jews?" Why did the God who created all that was, and is, and ever will be, single out one particular family, one clan, one tribe, and reveal that, while He may love all his children, He loves his special people with a special fervor and has chosen it to be the receptacle of his revelation to the entire human race?

To answer this, one must first consider the development of Judaism over the centuries. It is a misconception to believe that the Jews from the very beginning were monotheists, recognizing only one God over the entire world and that it was He who chose them for special favor, as well as special chastisement on occasion, out of all the families of the earth. In fact, however, the ancestors of the Jews were not monotheists. Like the other peoples of antiquity, the early Jews believed that each nation had its own god. At this time in history, each tribe or city-state venerated its own particular deity. The peoples worshipped their respective gods, and believed that their god sought to protect them and would lead them in battle against their enemies, bestowing upon them, when they were worthy, the gifts of fertility and prosperity. The early Jews believed that their God came to them in Egypt, where they were slaves. He

1

fought against their enemies, the rulers of Egypt and their gods, and enabled his people to emerge out of slavery and go up to battle the people of Canaan and their gods. Through the help of this deity the Jews were able to triumph and take possession of the land. This was a theology that all the peoples of the ancient world, including the Jews, understood and accepted.

In the sixth century B. C., however, the Jews and their theology were forced to come to grips with something quite new in their experience: Jerusalem had been destroyed by the Babylonians, the great Temple of the God of the Jews was sacked and burned, and many of the people were exiled from the land. According to the old theology shared by all of the ancients, this should have been interpreted as the defeat not only of a people, but of their God as well. The God of the Jews had been vanquished and dethroned, his place taken by the god of the victorious invader. This interpretation, though, did not take hold, because of the teaching of the prophet Jeremiah. Building upon the insights and teachings of his predecessors in the prophetic office, Jeremiah affirmed that the destruction of Jerusalem and the Temple, as well as the exile of the Jews, was the work of the very God whom the Jews worshipped as their own. The God of the Jews had not been defeated; rather, his will had been done and the disasters the Jews faced were the result of his judgment, executed upon those who had disobeyed the commandments of the moral law. Pray for the welfare of Babylon, Jeremiah wrote to the Jews who had been exiled there, for in its welfare you will find your welfare, and before long your God will bring you back to your home. In time the return to Jerusalem from the exile in Babylon did occur, and this enabled Jewish theologians and teachers to build upon and expand the concepts advocated by Jeremiah. Now, they taught, the God of the Jews was not only the God of the land from which the Jewish people had come, but He was as well God of all lands and all peoples. He remained most immediately the God of his people the Jews, but his power was now perceived to extend far beyond the land that was theirs. It extended, in fact, to the ends of the earth. All peoples and all lands were his, but the Jews were his special people and the land of the Jews his special land. This concept of the "chosenness" of the Jews is preserved not only in the religion of the Jews but in Christianity and Islam as well.

Every people wishes to believe that it is special in some way, so it is no wonder that, even in their new theology that now enthroned their God over all that is or will be, the Jews continued to believe that He remained in a special, loving relationship with them. The love of God for his people will never end, they were taught. (Without this teaching Judaism would never have persisted beyond the time of the ancients. With this teaching it may endure into eternity, if indeed it be true that God's love for the Jews is eternal.) Because they now believed themselves to be the special people of the One God of heaven and earth, the Jews came to think of themselves as "a people that dwells alone, not reckoning itself among the nations" (Numbers 23:9). And, in response, many of the other peoples of antiquity began to look upon the Jews as different and set apart.

The nameless prophet whose words are found in the latter part of the book of Isaiah taught that the nations would come to accept the God of the Jews as their divine ruler as well. They would stream to Jerusalem to pay tribute to Him and to his people:

> The wealth of Egypt and the merchandise of Ethiopia and the Sabeans, men of stature, shall come to you and be yours; they shall follow you; they shall come over in chains and bow down to you. They will make supplication to you, saying "God is with you only, and there is no other, no god besides him." (Isaiah 45:14)

Given this assumption of privilege, it is not difficult to understand that while many in the ancient world developed an admiration for the Jews and for the moral code that was an important part of their law, there were others who cultivated a fear and disdain for them. Because of their sense of separateness Jews were not universally regarded as a "lovable people."

After the return from Babylon, the religion of the Jews came to be based upon an explication of the sacred text promulgated by Ezra and the priestly caste around 450 B.C. (see p. 28.) A number of sects subsequently arose, each claiming to possess the proper understanding of the text and the legitimate authority to interpret and base legislation upon it. The sect of the Pharisees was the predecessor of what later came to be called Rabbinic Judaism, the ancestor of all the forms of Judaism that exist in the modern world. The Pharisees taught that the entire Jewish people, those who trace their descent from the biblical patriarchs as well as those from other nations who had embraced the God of the Jews and his law, constituted "Israel," the people of God with whom a divine covenant was in force. Individual Jews could be sinners and perhaps even entire groups of Jews could forsake their covenant responsibilities; but, said Pharisaic teaching, they were still part of "Israel" and could repent their shortcomings. Some of the other sects, though, maintained that only *they* constituted the "true Israel." Those Jews who rejected the true teaching, as interpreted by themselves, were not part of "Israel" and were no better than the vast multitudes of pagans who had no knowledge of God.

One of the Jewish sects that claimed to be the "true Israel" was the nascent Christian Church. The Church claimed that God had sent the savior Jesus to the Jews and that the majority of Jews had erred by rejecting or ignoring him. Though the apostle Paul portrayed the Church as a wild olive shoot grafted onto the cultivated tree of the Jewish people and wrote in Romans 11, "God has not cast away his people which He foreknew . . . and so all Israel shall be saved," the dominant view in the early Church was that God had rejected the Jews as his people except for that small number who had accepted Jesus. The theology of the Christian Church then evolved a doctrine that God had created a "new Israel" to replace the old, adding to the small number of Jewish followers of Jesus the much larger number of people from non-Jewish nations who accepted Jesus as lord and savior. This body, in the Church's view, constituted the "true Israel." In this manner did the non-Jewish world take its revenge upon the Jews for the claim that they alone had a knowledge of the true God and that they were his special people. The Jews had to contend with the assertion of the Church that they had been rejected by God and that the Church, composed in great measure of people who possessed no Jewish blood whatever, was now "Israel."

Some 600 years later Judaism had to contend with a similar phenomenon when Islam, the religion founded by Muhammad, proclaimed that it was the true heir of the patriarchs and prophets of Israel and that Muhammad was the "seal," the final and authoritative messenger sent to humanity by God. The Jews, said Islam, had been given a sacred book by God, but they (and the Christians, too) had misunderstood and misinterpreted it. In the judgment of Islam, the community founded by Muhammad supplanted the Jews as the true people of God when the Jews refused to accept Muhammad as the true and final prophet. Thus, Islam joined Christianity in rejecting the claim of the Jews that they were God's special people. Though Jews might well have been the chosen people in the past, both religions asserted, they now were rejected by God.

After biblical times, Jews for the most part came to live in lands where either Christians or Muslims were dominant, although the dispersion of the Jews had begun, of course, many centuries earlier. Many Jews voluntarily remained in Babylon after the end of the exile. Hundreds of thousands of Jews settled voluntarily in the developing cities of the hellenistic (Greek) world, such as Alexandria and Antioch, and later in Rome and in the Rhineland cities established by the Romans. In these places many Jews maintained their religious separateness from the people in whose midst they lived and voluntarily sent an annual tax for the support of the Temple in Jerusalem. When Christianity or Islam took control of the lands in which Jews lived, the people and the faith had to contend with the claims of these religions that they were the true heirs of the ancestors and prophets of the Jews, that they and not the Jews were the true "people of God." In response, Judaism developed a belief that emphasized that it would be vindicated in the end of days, that faithfulness to the teachings of the Hebrew Scriptures and the interpretations of the rabbis would result in the reward of a life in heaven after death and an eternal life on a renewed earth when the resurrection of the bodies of the just would take place. At that time, all flesh would see that, indeed, the Jews were God's special people, and the claims of those who denied this assertion would be destroyed. Thus, the "people that dwells alone" continued to dwell alone in an even more poignant and exaggerated way in the midst of populations that worshipped the God of the Jews and derived their religious doctrines from the Scriptures of the Jews. This is quite an important factor in the lives of many Jews even today.

The dispersion of the Jews from their ancestral land turned them, for the most part, into a city-dwelling people rather than a nation of peasants tilling the soil. The tendency to settle in the cities rather than in rural settings steered a number of Jews toward intellectual pursuits. This cultivation of intellectual abilities and interests was further strengthened by religious tradition. Worship services were integrated with the study and discussion of Scripture and the rabbinic commentaries, and laymen were expected to participate along with rabbis and scholars. Literacy thus received powerful encouragement, and Jewish men over the age of thirteen were expected to be able to lead the Hebrew services and read the sacred texts. In many communities in Europe and the Moslem world, Jewish intellectual interests went beyond religious concerns, and some Jews became quite prominent as physicians, poets, and philosophers.

When the French Revolution burst upon Europe in 1789, bringing with it the ideal of a common citizenship not predicated upon religious identity, the Jews as a whole readily embraced participation in the new opportunities open to them. Jews in Western and Central Europe entered the professions, the sciences, and the arts, and for a time it appeared that the Revolution's ideals of liberty, equality, and fraternity would sweep away all the bigotries and hatreds of past centuries.

The Revolution even influenced Jewish religious life. Various efforts at "reform" of the worship service and Jewish practices were made in Central Europe and spread to America during the immigrations of the midnineteenth century. "Reform" Judaism shortened the services, eliminated much of the Hebrew in favor of vernacular languages, promoted the equality of women in the religious sphere, eliminated specifically "Jewish" modes of dress both at worship and other activities, and modified the dietary restrictions of Jewish law. Traditionalists quite naturally opposed many aspects of reform, particularly when the philosophy behind reform came to embrace the "critical" approach of Protestant scholars who denied the divine inspiration of Scripture, regarding it as the product of historical development. Reform teaching also denied the Jewish expectation of a messianic ruler who would restore the kingdom of Israel and lead the Jews from the four corners of the earth to Jerusalem. In the view of the Reformers, the Jews should no longer consider themselves a separate nation, for they now were equal citizens of the lands in which they lived.

Just as many Jews did not embrace Reform, so, too, were there many Christians in Western and Central Europe who were not prepared to grant Jews civic and social equality. These were people who had not become reconciled to the ideals of the French Revolution: remnants of the aristocracy who lamented lost privileges; churchmen who decried the passing of "old-time religion," when knowing whom to hate was as important as knowing whom to love; merchants, artisans, and musicians who were wary of Jewish competition; elements of the underclass (*lumpenproletariat*) who were jealous of Jewish success. Among many of these people the doctrines of "anti-Semitism" took root. But anti-

Semitism went beyond mere opposition to the Jewish religion. It introduced the concept that there was something inherently noxious and evil in Jewish blood and that Jews were a contaminant of the culture and society in which they lived. The logical culmination of anti-Semitism was Nazism with its efforts to destroy all the Jews of Europe during the Second World War. The Jews at that time learned that the days of "liberty, equality, and fraternity" had not yet come and that reform or no, they remained "a people that dwells alone," though there were many who did what they could to ensure that they would dwell nowhere at all.

The response of the Jewish people to the anti-Semitism of the nineteenth century was Zionism, the doctrine that only the return of the people to its ancient homeland could solve the problem of the Jews. There had always been some Jews who settled in Palestine for religious reasons, but Zionism, founded by Theodore Herzl, took on the task of influencing the rulers of the world to support Jewish resettlement there. Great Britain received the League of Nations mandate to administer Palestine after the First World War. One of its responsibilities was to foster the development of a "Jewish national home." During these years, Jewish settlement increased and many communal and cultural institutions developed, but it was only with the advent of Nazism in Germany and the Second World War that Jewish resettlement of Palestine became a mass movement. The Jews released from the death camps of Europe after the war sought to go to the ancient land in large numbers. Arab nationalism opposed continued Jewish settlement, and the British relinquished their mandate over the land. The State of Israel came into being on the portions of Palestine under Jewish control on May 14, 1948, as Arab armies attempted to exterminate it at birth. The name "Israel" was chosen with deliberation, as an assertion that it is indeed the Jews who constitute the "true Israel."

Contemporary Judaism compares the Holocaust, the extermination of the Jews of Europe, to the torment and slavery of ancient Israel in Egypt. In like manner, some

Jews compare the creation of the State of Israel to the Exodus. The two pairs of events celebrate the redemptive power of God, who brought his people "from bondage to freedom, from subjugation to redemption, from sorrow to joy, from mourning to festivity, from darkness to great light" (*Haggada* of Passover).

The State of Israel defeated the Arab armies in 1948, but it was only in 1967, after another Arab invasion, that Israel was able to wrest control of the Old City of Jerusalem from Arab control. The Temple Mount was once again a Jewish possession, although the buildings on it were Muslim shrines constructed centuries ago to commemorate Muhammad's ascent to heaven from the sacred site. To a number of Orthodox Jews the State of Israel assumed even greater theological significance in 1967 since, they said, the return to the Temple Mount constituted "the beginning of the redemption" or the "footsteps of the Messiah." For the first time in 2,000 years, the world—and the Jews themselves—have to deal with the possibility of Jewish "triumphalism" and the interreligious turmoil that such an attitude can promote.

In the ensuing pages we will consider the doctrines and way of life that the religion of the Jews promulgates. We will present this material from a scientific and historical perspective, as well as from the standpoint of Orthodox Jewish tradition. There have been defections from Judaism during all of its history, but it has retained a tenacious hold on its people for thousands of years. Why have so many persevered, often in the face of hardship, persecution, or death, in the conviction that their people is indeed God's "special treasure," that He loves his people with an intense and eternal love that is unlike any other? Perhaps some readers will find some answers in the pages that follow.

CHAPTER TWO

Ancient Israel

The Patriarchs

The cradle of western civilization has been traced by historians and archeologists to the ancient city-states that flourished between the Tigris and Euphrates Rivers, the lands that were known in early times as Sumer and Akkad and, later, as the empires of Assyria and Babylonia. The ancestors of ancient Israel, according to the historical record preserved in the Bible, came from these lands. They were people who spoke a Semitic language (the linguistic family that includes Akkadian, Hebrew, Aramaic, and Arabic), and they were seminomadic shepherds. Historians include them among the Western Semite migrants of the eighteenth century B.C., who left the territory between the rivers seeking pastureland farther to the west in what was then called Canaan (in later years, Israel and Palestine).

The Bible personifies the ancestors of Israel as the patriarchs Abraham, Isaac, and Jacob, together with their wives and households. According to the book of Genesis, the God whom Abraham revered sent him on his journey to Canaan, "the land which I shall show you," and promised him that his descendants would become as numerous as the stars in the heavens and the sand upon the seashore and that they would become a blessing to all the families of the earth. The patriarchs lived peacefully in Canaan until a great famine devastated the land during the days of Jacob, following which he and his twelve sons crossed into Egypt with their households in search of food. According to the Genesis story, Joseph, the son of Jacob, had earlier become the ruler of the land second only to the king himself, and when Jacob and the rest of his family came, they were received with great honor and given fertile pastureland to hold as their own.

The family of Jacob that settled in Egypt is denominated in the Bible as either "Hebrews" or "Israel." *Hebrew* is understood as meaning "migrant." The word appears in Egyptian and Akkadian texts as *habiru* or *apiru*, where it is used as an appelation for a number of groups in addition to Israelites. *Israel* is an epithet bestowed upon Jacob in the book of Genesis. It is defined there as "he who strives with God." It came early on to signify all those who trace their descent from the patriarch Jacob and who preserve his spiritual legacy.

Moses and the Return to Canaan

The book of Exodus states that, after some years, "a new king arose in Egypt, who knew not Joseph." The new king is said to have enslaved the Israelites, putting them to work as the builders of royal cities. The Israelites, who by this time had come to number in the thousands, turned in their agony to the God of their ancestors. The Bible relates that an Israelite who had been raised in the royal palace came to be their savior. Moses, whose name is the same as the Eyptian word for "son," defied the ruler of Egypt and demanded that he let the people of Israel go free that they might serve the God of their ancestors. Pharaoh, the king of Egypt, vacillated and finally refused, so Egypt was smitten with plagues until Israel went forth "amid signs and wonders." The climactic sign was the crossing of the Red Sea and the drowning of all of Pharaoh's hosts as they came in pursuit. Most scholars date Moses about 1200 B.C.

While Moses maintained that it was the God of their ancestors who had sent him to lead Israel out of Egypt, it was Moses himself who, according to Exodus 6, revealed the true "name" of God to Israel. This is *Yahweh*, which most scholars derive from the Semitic root meaning "to be," and translate either as "the one who is" or "the one who causes to be"—i.e., "the sustainer." A fuller form of the divine name is "Yahweh of Hosts" (*sebaot*), meaning "sustainer of armies," referring to the armies of Israel or the host of heaven, or both. At a later period the name came to be considered too sacred to pronounce, perhaps even too filled with power to leave in the possession of ordinary people, so the use of the name *Yahweh* has dropped out of Judaism. In Hebrew texts of the Bible the consonants YHWH of *Yahweh* are combined with the vowels of *Adonai*, meaning "the Lord," and Jews have been taught from childhood that this hybrid form must be pronounced "Adonai." Some of the early Christian translators, however, did not realize this and they read the divine name as they found it written. This is the origin of the word *Jehovah*. Most Bible translations, both Jewish and Christian, translate *Yahweh* not as a proper name but as "the Lord." (In ordinary discourse, as distinct from prayer, even *Adonai* is too sacred to pronounce, according to Orthodox Judaism. Readers of these pages who wish to follow Orthodox practice should therefore pronounce the Divine Name as *haShem*, meaning "the Name," or as "the Lord.")

Moses not only led Israel out of Egyptian bondage; he also, according to the Bible, initiated all Israel into a covenant with Yahweh in the desert of Sinai. This covenant required that Israel would serve only Yahweh and no other deity. In return Yahweh would take Israel as his unique people and lead them in war to resettle the land of Canaan, where their ancestors had dwelt. The Bible elaborates this covenant in the form of the Ten Commandments. These stipulate several ethical requirements in addition to the prohibition of the worship of any other god besides Yahweh. Idolatry is forbidden; thus, images of Yahweh are unknown in ancient Israelite worship. Also, the observance of the seventh-day Sabbath is enjoined as a special sign of the covenant between Yahweh and his people. In Jewish teaching, not only were all Israelites then alive present at the moment of revelation at Sinai, but also the souls of those yet unborn, including those who would be born as Jews during the subsequent millennia as well as those who would come from without to embrace Judaism, were there to enter into the covenant and subscribe to it with the words, "We will do and we will hearken" (Exodus 24:7).

Moses functions in the Bible as Israel's liberator, as the prophet who introduced the people to its God, and as their judge and ruler until his death at the age of 120 years. (For this reason Jews wish each other long life with the words "until 120 years," since if even Moses had to be content with no more than that, so should we all.) It was his teaching to Israel that God himself should be their only King. Hereditary monarchy was unknown to Israel at this time, for all people were to be equal. It was only after Israel had become settled in Canaan, alongside other tribes who had kings, that monarchy developed. Israel in its early period sought to function as a family, with all of its people united by a tradition of common ancestry stemming from the patriarchs. (Some modern scholars maintain that the twelve tribes of Israel were not in reality descended from twelve sons of Jacob, but instead were groups of varied origins who shared a common faith in Yahweh as their God. If this is true, the tradition of common ancestry developed to create a more unified people, linked together not only by a common deity but by the patriarchs as well.)

It was only after Moses' death that, according to the Bible, Israel was ready to cross the Jordan River and invade the land of Canaan. Some scholars regard the penetration of Canaan as basically peaceful, the newcomers merging with the native Canaanites and learning the techniques of agriculture from them. Others give more credence to the Bible's portrayal of many bloody encounters between Israel and the Canaanites, with the latter becoming almost eliminated from the land. In recent years some scholars have concluded that a major portion of Israel was actually Canaanite in origin, people in rebellion against the feudal structure of the Canaanite city-states who developed an egalitarian social and religious system for themselves. Be that as it may, the Bible emphasizes that Israel was to root out the gods of the Canaanites, for Yahweh was not only a God of war but it was He who would bestow fertility on the land if his people offered worship and sacrifice to Him alone.

The book of Joshua relates that the men of Israel circumcised themselves at the Jordan River before entering Canaan, for after arriving in Egypt and thereafter they had been uncircumcised. We are able to surmise from this that Yahweh, the God of Israel, had come to be identified with El, the exalted Father-God of Canaanite religion (the name means "God" in Semitic languages). The Phoenicians, who were a Canaanite people, have left behind myths that speak of circumcision as a rite practiced in the cult of El. If Yahweh and El came to be regarded as the same deity, then the Bible's insistence that all traces of Canaanite worship be destroyed becomes even more understandable, for the Canaanites of this region and time were devoted not to El but to Baal, the son of the Father-God whom they believed had usurped the power of the Father over the land. The Bible denounces the worship of Baal time and again, and the struggle between Israel and the Canaanites is portrayed as a war between Yahweh and Baal. It may well be that Israel's conquest of Canaan brought that land once more into the domain of the deity who had been its Lord centuries before. Joshua 1:4 describes the ideal boundaries of the territory that, it was hoped, would be bestowed upon Israel by its God: "from the desert and Lebanon as far as the Great River, the river Euphrates—all the land of the Hittites to the Great Sea of the Setting Sun" (the Mediterranean). This was the land that lay between Egypt to the west and

Assyria and Babylonia to the east, the land that in early Canaanite religion had been the domain of El.

Although circumcision came to Israel from the Canaanite cult of El, which required those who wished to reside in the land to undergo this rite, the Bible, of course, does not describe it in this way. In the book of Genesis circumcision is commanded by Yahweh to Abraham as a sign of the covenant made by the deity with him and his descendants. While practiced by many peoples in both ancient and modern times, circumcision has come to be tenaciously cherished by the Jews to the present day. Jewish male infants are to be circumcised on their eighth day of life unless there is medical necessity for postponing it.

Israel's early years in Canaan are described in the book of Judges. These men (as well as one woman, Deborah) were not judicial figures, but instead charismatic leaders in war against various non-Israelite tribes. The Israelites also warred among themselves. Sacrifices were offered to Yahweh at the many "high places" or holy sites in the land, but the local cults of Baal persisted as well. According to the book of Judges, "every man did what was right in his own eyes." Conditions would eventually change, however, for a new challenge rose to confront Israel. Israel had been able to defeat the Canaanites, but the Philistines (from whom the name "Palestine" comes) were a different matter. These were the "Sea Peoples" who invaded Canaan from the Mediterranean and competed with Israel for the domination of the entire land. Fierce warriors, they had mastered the technology of working with iron.

The Kingdoms

"Give us a king to rule over us like all the nations" was a cry that came from many in Israel, because the loose confederacy of tribes spent as much energy warring among themselves as they did against outside enemies, and people were convinced that the better disciplined Philistines would overwhelm them. Saul, from the tribe of Benjamin, had a reputation as a brave and resourceful warrior, and he was anointed king. If the traditions preserved in the book of Samuel are accurate, after a time Saul began to exhibit signs of paranoia and suffer periods of depression. David, an acclaimed warrior from the tribe of Judah who had been an intimate of the king and his household, broke away from Saul to lead his own band of followers. When Saul and several of his sons had fallen in battle against the Philistines, David seized the opportunity to become king, a dignity that was ratified by the leaders of the various tribes of Israel. David was able to turn aside the Philistine menace against Israel, and it was he who merged the tribes of Israel into something like a unified people, at least for a time. He defeated Israel's enemies on all its frontiers and extended its military might as far as Damascus. According to tradition, David was also very devoted to Yahweh and, as the "sweet singer of Israel," wrote many of the poems found in the book of Psalms. Small wonder, then, that Judaism regards him to this day as the ideal king, the type of ruler for whom the righteous yearn.

David's most important accomplishment was perhaps his conquest of Jerusalem, because this city, according to Genesis 14, was the sanctuary of El, invoked there as "El the Most High." Yahweh, the God of Israel who had journeyed with his people out of Egypt and led them in battle against their many enemies, could now take residence in the holy place that Canaanite religion consigned to El, their most exalted deity. Yahweh and El were now one and the same, and Israel's claim to the land was indisputable. It was the God of this land who had given it to this people, and they would retain it forever if they remained devoted to Him. The people now had an eternal claim to the land, and David and his descendants, it was taught, would for eternity be kings over Israel if they remained true to Yahweh, God Most High. The Ark of Yahweh, which had accompanied the people of Israel on its desert journey and the armies of Israel when they went into battle, was brought by David into Jerusalem where, in celebration of its finding a home, the king "danced with all his might" before Yahweh.

David was followed on the throne of Israel by his son Solomon. Solomon inherited a prosperous kingdom, and Israel was a power to be reckoned with both politically and economically during his reign. In Jewish (as well as Islamic) folklore, Solomon appears as the master of all forms of wisdom, understanding the languages of animals and birds and subjecting even demons to his will. The Bible says also that he had 700 wives and 300 concubines. Inspired by his father's example, King Solomon expressed his devotion to Yahweh by building a magnificent Temple to Him in Jerusalem. There Solomon installed a new priesthood that served Yahweh with set rituals of sacrifice. (Israel's earlier priesthood was called "the Levites," from a Semitic root meaning "to escort," since they had escorted the Ark of Yahweh on its journeys. The Levites remained as priests in the many other sanctuaries of Yahweh throughout the land.)

King Solomon, however, does not appear to have been beloved by all his people. He favored his own tribe of Judah to the detriment of the other tribes of Israel, and he imposed a corvée, or levy of unpaid labor for public works, upon the men of the kingdom. After Solomon's death the leaders of the tribes approached his son as he was about to be proclaimed king, and they asked if he would lighten the burdens that his father had imposed upon the people. His reply, according to the Bible, was this: "My father chastised you with whips, but I will chastise you with scorpions." The elders of ten of the twelve tribes thereupon refused to accept Solomon's son as their king. They severed their connection with the dynasty of David and set up a new and truncated kingdom of Israel. Only the tribe of Judah and the contiguous tribe of Benjamin, with the royal city of Jerusalem in its territory, remained loyal to the house of David. They constituted the kingdom of Judah.

The people of the kingdom of Israel continued to regard Yahweh as their God, though they were told by Jeroboam, their first king, that they should cease to venerate Jerusalem. Instead, Jeroboam established temples near the southern boundary of the kingdom and in the north. No royal dynasty was ever able to establish itself for any extended period of time, since many of the kings, who were basically military leaders, were murdered and usurpers seized the throne. The kingdom of Israel came to an end in 721 B.C., when the Assyrians conquered it and exiled its people far to the north. The exiles ceased to retain their identity or their religion and are remembered in tradition as the "ten lost tribes of Israel." The Bible relates that the Assyrians brought foreign peoples to settle the land. These mingled with the few Israelites who had not gone into exile and adopted the worship of Yahweh. They are referred to in Jewish sources as the Samaritans (after Samaria, the capital city of Israel). A few hundred Samaritans exist to this day in Shechem, the ancient city that is today known as Nablus.

The kingdom of Judah, though it had fewer natural resources than Israel, was much more stable than its neighbor and remained under the rule of the dynasty of David for its entire existence. The Assyrians besieged Jerusalem in 701 B.C. In the words of an inscription of the Assyrian king Sennacherib, "He [the king of Judah] I shut up in Jerusalem, his royal city, like a bird in a cage." The siege was not successful, however, since the Assyrian forces withdrew to deal with disturbances elsewhere in the empire. Judah thus maintained its existence for a time, unlike the kingdom of Israel. In 621 B.C. a major religious reformation was promulgated by King Josiah of Judah. According to the book of Kings, Josiah based his reforms on a book of religious law that had been discovered during a renovation of the Temple. Scholars are convinced that this refers to the book of Deuteronomy and its requirement that there be only one sanctuary in the land where sacrifice was to be offered to Yahweh. In the language of the book itself, there was to be but one place where Yahweh would "cause His name to dwell." Accordingly, Josiah closed down all the other sanctuaries of Yahweh in the land, including those hallowed by association with the ancient patriarchs. Sacrifice was to be offered only in the Temple of Jerusalem, to which all male Judean adults were to come with their offerings on the three pilgrimage festivals each year. The priests who had served in the other sanctuaries were brought to Jerusalem. There they served not as priests (who received and offered the sacrifices) but in a subordinate class, called Levites, that assisted the priests in the maintenance of the Temple and its worship. Both priests and Levites were supported by tithes, or taxes levied upon agricultural products and flocks belonging to the populace at large. The priests of the Temple came to be regarded as descendants of Aaron, the brother of Moses. The Levites were defined as distant kinsmen of the priests within the tribe of Levi. Even though the sacrificial cult ended in 70 A.D., traditional Judaism to this day preserves these distinctions within the Jewish people. A Jew is either *kohen* ("priest"), *levi* ("Levite"), or *yisrael* ("Israelite," an ordinary Jew).

Josiah's reformation involved not only the closing of all the sanctuaries other than those in Jerusalem, but also a thorough cleansing of the cult in Jerusalem itself. He destroyed the cult objects that had been dedicated to the worship of the sun and to Baal, broke down the houses of the prostitutes that had been part of the fertility rites centering about Baal, and defiled the altars that Solomon had built for the deities of the neighboring peoples. (Though Yahweh had always insisted that Israel was to worship Him exclusively, the common theology of the ancient Near East tolerated the worship of several deities, and only those who were fanatical in their devotion to Yahweh insisted otherwise.) Josiah embraced the exclusive service of Yahweh with a vengeance. By centralizing all sacrifice to Yahweh in Jerusalem, the king and the priests of Yahweh could exert total control over the forms that worship took. Judaism was on the way to becoming a pure monotheism, one in which the reality of all other gods besides Yahweh was denied.

When Josiah was slain in battle, the end was near for the kingdom of Judah. Babylonia was now the imperial power in the region and Judah paid tribute to it. The kings who succeeded Josiah thought that through alliance with Egypt they could throw off the Babylonian yoke. They thought, too, that Yahweh would protect his people, that He would never allow his Temple, his land, his beloved dynasty of David to remain for long under the rule of foreigners. The prophet Jeremiah ridiculed these beliefs and insisted that Yahweh was the power behind Babylon, that it was his will that Judah submit to its imperial rule. Jeremiah was right, both historically and in religious terms, but those in authority did not listen to him. In 586 B.C. the Babylonians destroyed Jerusalem and the Temple, put an end to the rule of the dynasty of David, and exiled the leading citizens to Babylon, leaving only "the poorest of the land to be vine dressers and plowmen." The kingdom of Judah was no more, and the religion of the Jews was to assume a new form.

The Prophets

It was the work of the prophets who lived during the existence of the kingdoms that enabled the religion of Yahweh to survive the destruction of the kingdom of Judah. Without the prophetic teachings, the Judeans exiled to Babylon would have adopted the gods of Babylon and, like all the other peoples of the ancient Near East, would have eventually lost their distinctive national identity. The prophets taught, however, that it was not Yahweh who had been defeated by the various calamities that the people had suffered. Yahweh rather had been vindicated, because it was He who had authorized their punishment. They had disobeyed his law, a law whose primary demands, according to the prophets, were ethical in nature rather than ritualistic. They had not changed their ways, though the prophets had come to warn them. Therefore He allowed their enemies to defeat them.

Prophets were not always teachers of ethics, nor were they primarily foretellers of the future. We find the profession of prophet in Israel from the time of the Judges, and there were prophets among other Semitic peoples as well. A prophet was a man, or occasionally a woman, who in a state of ecstasy believed that he received revelations from a deity. Sometimes prophets were hired for pay; at other times they delivered their messages gratuitiously. Some prophets operated in guilds under the direction of a prophetic master; others were solitary individuals who pursued other occupations until those times when "the spirit of God" would inspire them. Some prophets were officials attached to the courts of the kings; others were violently opposed to the rulers of their day.

In the Bible we first find an ethical emphasis in the message of a prophet in the person of Nathan, who was attached to David's court. He denounced the king for his adultery with Bathsheba and his subsequent arrangement to send her husband off to death in battle so that she would be free to marry the king. Elijah, too, in the days of Ahab, king of Israel, denounced the king and his wife Jezebel for the judicial murder of Naboth, based upon false testimony, and the king's confiscation of the old man's coveted vineyard. Some prophets told the kings what they wanted to hear; others, however, walked in the way of Nathan and Elijah and shaped and formed the religious tradition.

The first prophet whose actual words are preserved in a biblical book was Amos, who came to the royal temple of the kingdom of Israel about 750 B.C. to deliver his message. Assyria would devastate the land, he said,

> Because you trample upon the poor and take from him exactions of wheat, you have built houses of hewn stone but you shall not live in them; you have planted vineyards but you shall not drink their wine. . . . I (Yahweh) hate, I despise your feasts, and I take no delight in your solemn assemblies. Though you offer Me burnt offerings and cereal offerings I will not accept them. The peace offerings of your fatted beasts I will not look upon. Take

away from Me the noise of your songs; to the melody of your harps I will not listen. Rather let justice roll down like water and righteousness like a mighty stream. (Amos 5)

Hosea followed Amos in the kingdom of Israel, inveighing against the worship of Baal. He compared Israel to an adulterous wife who leaves her husband (Yahweh) to join her lover (Baal). At last she realizes that it was Yahweh who was able to provide her with "the grain, the wine, the oil," and she seeks to return to Him. If she truly repents her deeds, Yahweh will take her back. To dramatize his message, Hosea actually married a prostitute. He, too, stressed the ethical dimension, believing that the cult of Baal, with its concern for rites of fertility, ignored ethical concerns:

There is no faithfulness or kindness and no knowledge of God in the land. There is, instead, false swearing, lying, killing, stealing and adultery; they break all bounds and murder follows murder. Therefore the land mourns and all who dwell in it languish, even the beasts of the field and the birds of the air, and the fish of the sea are taken away. (Hosea 4)

Micah prophesied in the kingdom of Judah during the time of the Assyrian threat. His message was this:

Hear this, you heads of the house of Jacob and rulers of the house of Israel, who abhor justice and pervert equity, who build Zion with blood and Jerusalem with wrong. Its heads give judgment for a bribe, its priests teach for hire; its prophets divine for money. Yet they lean upon Yahweh and say, "Is not Yahweh in our midst? No evil can befall us." Therefore because of you Zion shall be plowed as a field; Jerusalem shall become a heap of ruins, and the mountain of Yahweh's house a wooded height. (Micah 3)

Micah is the prophet who provided what is perhaps the most oft-quoted vision of what religion should be:

> With what shall I come before Yahweh, and bow myself before God on high? Shall I come before Him with burnt offerings, with calves a year old? Will Yahweh be pleased with thousands of rams, with myriads of rivers of oil? Shall I give my first-born for my transgression, the fruit of my body for the sin of my soul? He has told you, O man, what is good, and what Yahweh requires of you. Only to do justice, and to love kindness, and to walk humbly with your God. (Micah 6)

The prophet Isaiah was a contemporary of Micah's. During at least part of his career, he was a court prophet, called upon by the king when he wished to know the will of Yahweh. His message was like that of his predecessors:

> When you come to appear before Me, who requires of you this trampling of my courts? Bring no more vain offerings; incense is an abomination to Me. New moon and sabbath and the calling of assemblies—I cannot endure iniquity along with solemn assembly. Your new moons and appointed feasts I hate. They have become a burden to Me, I am weary of bearing them. When you spread forth your hands I will hide my eyes from you. Though you make many prayers I will not listen, for your hands are full of blood. Wash yourselves, make yourselves clean; remove the evil of your doings from before my eyes. Cease to do evil, learn to do good; seek justice, correct oppression; defend the fatherless, plead for the widow. (Isaiah 1)

Many scholars think that the book of Deuteronomy was composed under the influence of the prophets. It contains many laws that serve to protect the poor, and its centralization of sacrifice in Jerusalem helped to purify the religion of Yahweh. The prophet Jeremiah lived during King Josiah's reformation and continued his career through the destruction of Jerusalem by Babylon and beyond. He is the only prophet who has preserved some of the details of his life in the book that bears his name. Imprisoned and beaten on numerous occasions, he nonetheless persisted in declaring to all who would listen that Yahweh wished Judah to submit to the suzerainty of Babylon. Those who opposed him, including prophets who made a career of telling the kings what they wanted to hear, branded him a traitor and assured the ruler that Yahweh would surely defend his Temple and his city. Jeremiah wished that he could resign the prophetic office and live an unassuming life, but the word of Yahweh that was within him was a consuming passion:

Yahweh, You have seduced me and I was seduced. You are stronger than I, and You have prevailed. I am become a laughingstock all day long; everyone mocks me. Whenever I speak I cry out, I shout, "Violence and destruction!" The word of Yahweh has become for me a reproach and a derision all day long. If I say, "I will not mention Him or speak any more in his name," there is in my heart as it were a burning fire shut up in my bones. I am weary with holding it in, and I cannot. I hear many whispering. Terror is on all sides. "Denounce him, let us denounce him" say all my familiar friends, watching for my fall. "Perhaps he will be deceived, then we can overcome him and take our revenge on him." But Yahweh is with me as a dreaded warrior; therefore my persecutors will stumble and will not overcome me. They will be greatly shamed, for they will not succeed. Their eternal dishonor will never be forgotten. (Jeremiah 20)

The prophet was vindicated when Jerusalem was destroyed. His work continued, however. It was he who was responsible, perhaps even singlehandedly, for the preservation of the faith of the Jews in exile in Babylon and for the future of the people.

Exile and Return

Jeremiah sent this letter from Jerusalem to the exiles who had been deported to Babylon:

Thus says Yahweh of hosts, the God of Israel, to all the exiles whom I have sent from Jerusalem to Babylon. Build houses and live in them; plant gardens and eat their produce. Take wives and have sons and daughters; take wives for your sons and give your daughters in marriage, that they may bear sons and daughters. Multiply there and do not decrease. And seek the welfare of the city where I have sent you into exile and pray to Yahweh on its behalf, for in its welfare you will find your welfare. (Jeremiah 29)

He went on to say that the exile would last some seventy years, but then their descendants would be able to return to Jerusalem. The prophet with these words was teaching a true monotheism; that is, Yahweh had not been defeated, even though his people had been defeated. Moreover, his power extended to Babylon itself and He would eventually redeem the Jews if they remained true to Him. The growth of a monotheism of this type became possible, it seems, with the advent of the great empires that dominated the Near East. First Assyria, then Babylon, and thereafter Persia assumed dominion over what seemed to be almost the entire known world. If there could be a universal empire, then it followed that there was a universal God who could bring this empire into being. Yahweh, although He was especially the God of the Jews, thus came to be understood as the divine King of the entire earth, and worship could be offered to Him anywhere, not just in Judah or Israel.

Ezekiel was a prophet, probably a disciple of Jeremiah's, who lived among the exiles in Babylon. He emphasized that Yahweh was making of the Jews a holy people, one that would emerge from the crucible of adversity to be forever worthy of God's blessing.

I will make a covenant of peace with them; it shall be an everlasting covenant with them; I will bless and multiply them and set my sanctuary in their midst forevermore. . . . Then the nations will know that I Yahweh sanctify Israel, when my sanctuary is in their midst forevermore. (Ezekiel 37)

Ezekiel also stressed that each person, rather than the people as a collective, would be judged for his acts and rewarded or punished accordingly. This made possible the later teaching that, in the case of those who had not received their just deserts on earth, reward or punishment would be meted out even after death.

In 538 B.C. Cyrus of Persia overthrew the Babylonian Empire and, in accordance with his policy of allowing as much cultural independence as possible to the many peoples who made up the empire, he gave permission to the Jews in Babylon to return to Jerusalem and rebuild the Temple. Jeremiah's words thus came true. An anonymous prophet who lived during this thrilling time is called by scholars "the Second Isaiah," since his words constitute the second portion of the book of Isaiah. He came to the people with a message of comfort:

Comfort, comfort my people, says your God. Speak tenderly to Jerusalem and cry out to her that her time of service is ended, that her iniquity is pardoned, that she has received from Yahweh's hand double for all her sins. A voice cries, In the wilderness prepare the way of Yahweh, make straight in the desert a highway for our God. Every valley shall be lifted up, and every mountain and hill be made low; the crooked shall be made straight and the rough places a plain. And the glory of Yahweh shall be revealed, and all flesh shall see it together, for the mouth of Yahweh has spoken. (Isaiah 40)

The Second Isaiah was an uncompromising monotheist, insisting that Yahweh, God of Israel, held in his hand all

divine power in heaven and on earth and that the deities of
other nations were but figments of the imagination. He
defined Israel, the Jewish people, as the witnesses to Yahweh's
power and existence. Israel was the servant of Yahweh,
leading the peoples of the earth to the worship of the One
God who "forms light and creates darkness, makes peace
and creates evil" (Isaiah 45:7). It is quite possible that the
prophet was influenced by the Zoroastrian religion of the
Persians, which in its pure and essential form was monotheistic, and that he equated Yahweh with the deity that Cyrus
worshipped. The Persians, of course, would not necessarily
have agreed that Israel was the unique people of this One
God and that it was the end of Israel's exile that signified
this truth to the world.

Although Cyrus authorized the return of the Jews to
Jerusalem, relatively few of them seized the opportunity.
Many Jews remained in Babylon and spread out into the
cities between the Tigris and Euphrates. A large Jewish
community continued to exist there for 2,500 years. The
first group of Jews who returned to Jerusalem was led by a
descendant of David, but there are no records or even
traditions that reveal what became of him. The reconstitu-
ted community in Jerusalem came under the control of the
Temple priesthood. Under their leadership a Temple was
built on the site of the old one and sacrifices were restored,
although the Temple did not compare in size or splendor
with the one that had been destroyed. Priests assumed both
religious and political leadership, representing the community in its relationships with the Persian overlords. Another
group of Jews came from Babylon about 450 B.C. Their
leader was Ezra, a priest and scholar who, according to
most modern scholars, is primarily responsible for reestab-
lishing the Jews of Jerusalem on a firm foundation as a
community and laying the basis for Judaism as a religious
faith that has persisted to the present day. It is Ezra who
was responsible for the prohibition of intermarriage that is
so much a part of traditional Judaism. Although the Jews
and Israelites prior to his time intermarried quite routinely

with the neighboring peoples, Ezra forbade it for fear that mingling the seed of the holy people with other nations would compromise its pure monotheistic faith (Ezra 9).

The Bible describes how Ezra convoked a great assembly of all the Jews and read to them "the book of the law of Moses . . . reading from the book, from the law of God, clearly; and they gave the sense, so that the people understood the reading" (Nehemiah 8). Modern scholars are convinced that this event describes the promulgation of the Torah (the "five books of Moses") in the form that it exists to the present day. Although tradition insists that the Torah comes from the time of Moses, the fact that the people wept in agitation upon hearing Ezra read about certain ritual requirements indicates to some modern scholars that at least some portions of the text were new. (The word *torah* actually means "teaching," although the conventional translation from ancient times has been "law.") Other evidence that the Torah as such comes from the time of Ezra is provided by the Samaritan version of the Torah, which made its appearance at about the same time. If the Torah had actually been produced by Moses and known to all Israel for over 700 years, the Samaritans would not have been able to present an alternative version and claim that it, and not the Jewish one, was genuine. The major difference between the Samaritan text and the Jewish one is that the former stipulates that the central sanctuary of God is to be located not in Jerusalem but on Mount Gerizim, the sacred mountain near the Samaritan city of Shechem. Scholars agree that the Jewish text of the Torah is older than the Samaritan one. While the Samaritan Torah specifies that the sanctuary shall be located on Mount Gerizim, the Jewish text does not mention Jerusalem. It says merely that God would choose a place where "his name might dwell."

With the promulgation of the Torah, the character of the Jews as a people became profoundly changed. Formerly they had been in many respects like all the other peoples of the ancient world, following the instruction of their priests in religious matters because they believed that only the priests were knowledgeable about such matters. Now, however, the Jews as a people were given a text that was to be the property of all Jews, laity as well as priests. The sacrifices of the Temple were still in the domain of the priesthood, but all Jews were commanded to develop an understanding of the scriptural text. The Jews, at least ideally, were to become a "people of the Book." The priests were supposed to be teachers of the Torah, but the laity developed its scholars as well, and various schools of interpreting the Torah arose. Literacy, if not universal, became widespread among men and even a few women.

The promulgation of the Torah brought with it an end to prophecy, or at least the kind of prophecy that was considered legitimate by religious authority. In Jewish teaching the last prophets were those who lived as the exile was coming to an end. Once an authoritative sacred text became available, prophets were no longer necessary. In fact, they were even dangerous, since prophets were people who thought that God spoke through them. The teaching of religious authorities came to be that God spoke through the Torah. In place of prophets there were the interpreters of the Torah, the scholars, or, as they came to be called in later years, the rabbis.

Before the time of Ezra modern scholars speak of "the religion of Israel" or "the religion of Yahweh." From Ezra onward, however, they speak of "Judaism," the religion of the Judeans—or Jews—based upon the interpretation of the Torah. The love affair of the Jews with matters of the intellect had begun.

CHAPTER THREE

The Hebrew Scriptures

The Hebrew Scriptures, called in Christian tradition the Old Testament, consists of three parts: Torah, Prophets, and Writings. The collection as a whole is referred to in Hebrew as the *Tanak,* an acronym derived from the initial letters of the three divisions. The various books in the Scriptures were not written in chronological order. Modern scholarship maintains that many of the books in the Prophets were written before the books that comprise the Torah. Canonization, however—the definition by Jewish religious authority that certain books are holy or inspired—was chronological. First the Torah was canonized; later, the collection comprising the Prophets; and at a still later date, the books that make up the Writings.

Torah

The word *torah* is translated "teaching," "law," "the Five Books of Moses," or "Pentateuch." While in a technical sense it refers to the five books that make up this section of the Hebrew Bible, in Jewish religious discourse the word is often used to mean all of Jewish teaching, from its origin to the present day. Modern scientific scholarship links the promulgation and canonization of the Torah to Ezra about

450 B.C. Traditional Judaism, however, has always insisted that it is the revelation of God to Moses, who then brought it to all Israel. All Israel is supposed to have heard the Ten Commandments spoken by God at Mount Sinai fifty days after the Exodus from Egypt. Thereafter God is supposed to have dictated the rest of the Torah to Moses, who wrote it down in scroll form. Unlike the later prophets, to whom God spoke in dreams or while they were in an ecstatic state, Moses is said to have heard the voice of God and spoken to Him as one person does to another, "face to face." Traditional teaching is unclear whether God dictated the Torah all at once or whether He revealed it to Moses section by section during the years that Israel wandered in the desert before entering Canaan, the Promised Land.

The books of the Torah consist of the following:

- *Genesis*—concerning the creation of the world and the human race; genealogies of the patriarchs of humanity before Noah's flood; the story of the flood; the stories of the patriarchs from Noah to Abraham; the traditions clustered about Abraham, Isaac, and Jacob; the journey of the Israelites to Egypt.

- *Exodus*—concerning Israel's enslavement in Egypt; God's call to Moses; the Exodus and the crossing of the Red Sea; the Ten Commandments and other civil and criminal laws; the apostasy of Israel with the golden calf while Moses was on Mount Sinai; the building of the portable sanctuary that was carried through the desert.

- *Leviticus*—concerning the types of sacrifices to be offered in the sanctuary; dietary laws; the rules for purification after childbirth; the rules of separation for lepers and menstruating women; the ritual for the Day of Atonement; forbidden sexual contacts; the ethical requirements for a state of holiness (including the commandment to "love your neighbor as yourself"); the rules of purity for the priests; the festivals, sabbatical years (occurring every seven years) when debts are to be canceled, fields are to lie fallow, and those who are in slavery for debt are to be freed, and jubilee years (occurring every fifty years), when all land is to revert to the family of its original Israelite owner; blessings and curses for obedience and disobedience of divine law.

• *Numbers*—concerning the census of the tribes; the ordeal of bitter waters for a woman accused of adultery; the nazirite vow (a discipline in which one gives up cutting his hair and drinking wine); the offerings of the tribes at the dedication of the altar; the order of march of the tribes on leaving Sinai; the quails sent by God when the people demanded meat; the spies who brought a pessimistic report about Israel's prospects of conquering Canaan; Israel's defeat by a band of Canaanites because they did not have faith that God could lead them to victory; Korah's rebellion against Moses and Aaron and the miraculous signs from Yahweh that He had truly chosen Aaron as his priest; the rules for preparing the red heifer (whose ashes were to be sprinkled upon one who had become defiled by contact with a dead body); Israel's defeat of two kings east of the Jordan; the story and oracles of Balaam (the heathen prophet hired to curse Israel who was forced by Yahweh to bless them instead); Israel's seduction to idolatry by the Midianites and the plague that broke out in punishment; the slaughter of the Midianites in revenge; the revelation to Moses that daughters have the right to inherit from their father if he has no sons; the settlement of two and a half tribes of Israel east of the Jordan River; the delineation of the boundaries of Canaan to be occupied by Israel; the provision for cities to be given to the Levites and for cities of refuge (where one who had accidentally killed someone could find asylum and be safe from the vengeance of the kin of him who had been killed).

• *Deuteronomy*—concerning Moses' reviews of the journeys and the wars of Israel; the Ten Commandments;

the commandment to love Yahweh "with all your heart and all your soul and all your might"; the law of the single sanctuary where Yahweh would cause his name to dwell; the prohibition of idolatry; dietary laws; the sabbatical year, the festivals, and various civil and criminal laws; the provision that when Israel went into Canaan the tribes would ascend the two sacred mountains in Shechem to hear the Levites recite the blessings and curses for keeping or rejecting the law of God; Israel's being urged to "choose life" rather than death by loving God and living by his law; Moses' farewell to Israel and his death.

While Orthodox Judaism teaches that these five books of the Torah, in their received Hebrew text, were revealed by God to Moses, the non-Orthodox forms of Judaism accept the insights and approaches of modern biblical scholarship. Linguists and historians utilizing scientific principles have developed various theories about the composition of the Torah. The proposal that has been most widely accepted by both Jewish and Christian scholars is called the documentary hypothesis. According to this theory, the Torah is an amalgamation of four texts, which the scholars call *J, E, D,* and *P*. The *J* document, they say, comes from Judah about the time of Solomon and refers to God most often as "Yahweh" (spelled *Jahweh* in German and other languages, whence the designation *J*). The *E* document comes from the kingdom of Israel and refers to God as "Elohim" (a Hebrew term for God or gods in the plural). The *D* document consists of Deuteronomy and certain portions of the other books. The *P* document is the work of the Priestly caste during the Babylonian exile and thereafter; it is the largest of the four hypothetical sources and the one into which the other three have been incorporated. Editors or redactors among the priests wove the four source texts together into the Torah text presented by Ezra to the Jerusalem community.

(Rabbis of the non-Orthodox branches of Judaism are all familiar with the documentary hypothesis. Some accept it wholeheartedly, while others are not so sure. The Jewish laity, by and large, does not know much about this type of scholarly research and many of them, even if they are not particularly religious, know only the traditional view that God gave the Torah to Israel "by the hand of Moses.")

Prophets

The second section of the Hebrew Bible, the Prophets, was presumably canonized shortly after Ezra's promulgation of the Torah, but no information has been preserved concerning when this was done, or where, or by whom. In addition to the texts of some of the prophetic figures themselves, this division of Scripture includes a number of historical books. In Jewish teaching, all of these texts are deemed to have been written by people endowed with the "spirit of prophecy."

The books of the Prophets consist of the following:

- *Joshua*—concerning traditions about the conquest of Canaan under the leadership of Joshua, successor to Moses.

- *Judges*—concerning the charismatic warrior figures who led individual tribes of Israel, or coalitions of tribes, against their enemies.

- *I and II Samuel*—concerning the prophet Samuel's leadership of Israel as the Philistine threat made its appearance; the choice of Saul as the first king; the story of David's heroic deeds, his accession to the throne, and the events during his reign (told from the perspective of a strong partisan of David and his dynasty).

- *I and II Kings*—concerning Solomon's reign; the division of the kingdom into Judah and Israel; an enumeration of the rulers of these states, together with the salient events of their respective reigns, up to the end of the kingdom of Israel in 721 B.C., and the end of the kingdom of Judah in 586 B.C. (The writer evaluates each king by the standards of Deuteronomy—that is, did he or did he not eliminate the worship of gods other than Yahweh and restrict sacrifice to Yahweh to the sanctuary in Jerusalem.)

- *Isaiah*—the words of Isaiah from the eighth century B.C., and the words of the "Second Isaiah," who lived as the Babylonian Exile was coming to an end.

- *Jeremiah*—the words of the prophet who lived through the destruction of Jerusalem by Babylon.

- *Ezekiel*—the words of the prophet among the exiles in Babylon.

- *The Twelve*—smaller collections of the words and careers of other prophets who lived in Israel or Judah: Hosea, Joel, Amos, Obadiah, Jonah, Micah, Nahum, Habakkuk, Zephaniah, Haggai, Zechariah, and Malachi. (The last three prophets lived in Jerusalem among the exiles who had returned from Babylon; after them there are no other prophets.)

Writings

The third part of the Hebrew Bible, the Writings, was put together over a long period of time. Some books were not included in the canon until an assembly of rabbis near the end of the first century A.D. declared them to be sacred scripture. According to modern scholars, a number of books in the Writings are much later than the time of the return from Babylon, when prophecy is supposed to have ceased. In traditional Judaism, however, these books all are adjudged to have been the work of people endowed with the spirit of prophecy and hence very old. The books in the Writings are considered to be less sacred than the books included in the Prophets. Although the books of the Prophets are deemed to have been written under direct inspiration from God through dreams or while in a state of trance, the books in the Writings are supposed to be the work of prophets writing in a more normal or mundane manner.

The books in the Writings consist of the following:

- *Psalms*—traditionally associated with David, the book of Psalms was without doubt considered sacred before there was any formalized collection of the Writings. Some of the psalms are personal prayers and meditations; others are from the worship at the Temple.

- *Proverbs*—ascribed to Solomon, Proverbs is a book of aphorisms and wise advice about life and its everyday challenges. Similar collections are known from other areas of the ancient Near East.

- *Job*—a drama about divine justice and the great question, "Why do the righteous suffer?"

- *Song of Songs*—a collection of erotic poetry that came to be considered sacred because it was interpreted as an allegory about God's love for Israel; ascribed to Solomon.

- *Ruth*—a story about a Moabite woman who embraced the God of Israel and his people, and became an ancestor of David.

- *Lamentations*—elegies over the destruction of Jerusalem by Babylon; traditionally ascribed to Jeremiah.

- *Ecclesiastes*—philosophical meditations about the futility of life by Kohelet, "king in Jerusalem." Modern scholars find a Greek influence, while tradition says that Kohelet was Solomon in his old age. (He is supposed to have written Song of Songs while young and lusty, and Proverbs in middle age.)

- *Esther*—a humorous story about the deliverance of the Jews of Persia from a plot to destroy them. It is the basis for the carnival holiday of Purim and is the latest book to be admitted to the canon of the Scriptures.

- *Daniel*—visions and interpretations of the end of days attributed to Daniel. Modern scholars date it at the time of the persecutions leading up to the revolt of the Maccabees in 168 B.C..

- *Ezra and Nehemiah*—records and accounts of the return from Babylon and the reconstruction of Jerusalem.

- *I and II Chronicles*—genealogies and accounts from the time of Adam through the history of Israel and Judah to the end of the Babylonian exile, written from the perspective of the Jerusalem priesthood.

Apocrypha, Septuagint, Targum

The rabbis who decided which books to include in the Writings also decided, naturally enough, that certain other books were to be excluded. These books do not constitute a formal collection, but they are known as the Apocrypha (from the Greek for "hidden away"). Some of them advocated doctrines of which the rabbis disapproved. Others dealt with events so long after the stipulated close of prophecy that it was impossible to pretend that they had been written earlier. Although these books are not included in the Hebrew Bible, they have fortunately been preserved in a Greek version and are considered inspired scripture by the Roman Catholic and Eastern Orthodox branches of Christianity. These churches derive their Old Testament from the ancient translation into Greek that retains these so-called apocryphal books.

The first language into which the Hebrew Bible was translated was Greek. This version is called the *Septuagint*, from the Greek for "seventy," since, according to legend, it was the work of seventy scholars. It was done for the benefit of the large Jewish community of Alexandria, in Egypt. The Jews of Alexandria were Greek-speaking, and very few of them retained any knowledge of Hebrew. The Septuagint version of the Torah was prepared before 250 B.C., with the other books translated over the next two centuries.

No ancient Jewish manuscripts of the Septuagint have been preserved; only texts by Christian copyists are extant. These texts do not preserve the threefold division of the Scriptures into Torah, Prophets, and Writings. The Greek version utilized by the Christian Church mixes the books that constitute the Writings in the Hebrew Scriptures with the Apocrypha—books that do not even exist in the Hebrew canon—and inserts them into the books that in the Hebrew version constitute the Prophets. Thus, in the Greek version, some of the prophetic books close the Old Testament, leading the reader into the specifically Christian Scriptures (the New Testament), which in Christian doctrine fulfills prophecies contained in the Old Testament.

It is apparent, though, that the organizing principle underlying the order of the books in the Septuagint is in actuality quite logical: (1) the books of the Torah, (2) historical books, (3) poetic and philosophical books, (4) the books of the prophets. Since they are based upon the Greek text, Roman Catholic and Eastern Orthodox editions of the Bible include the Apocrypha in their Old Testament. (These books, however, are styled "deutero-canonical," implying that they may possess a somewhat lesser degree of inspiration than the other books of Scripture.) Protestant translations of the Bible, which are based upon the Hebrew text, do not include the Apocrypha, although they do retain the ancient Christian tradition of putting prophetical books at the end of the Old Testament so that they lead into the gospels and the other books that make up the New Testament. Jewish Bibles differ from those used by Christians in that they include only the books that were transmitted in Hebrew, the sacred language (though two books contain some chapters in Aramaic), and they retain the tripartite division of the books into Torah, Prophets, and Writings. (Jewish Bibles, of course, do not include the New Testament.)

Ancient Jewish translations of the Hebrew Scriptures were done in Aramaic. This Semitic language is akin to Hebrew and was the ordinary language of daily discourse in Palestine from at least the first century B.C. and in the large Jewish

THE BOOKS OF THE GREEK OLD TESTAMENT

Genesis
Exodus
Leviticus
Numbers
Deuteronomy
Joshua
Judges
Ruth
I Kings (I Samuel)
II Kings (II Samuel)
III Kings (I Kings)
IV Kings (II Kings)
I Chronicles
II Chronicles
*I Esdras
II Esdras (Ezra-Nehemiah)
*Tobit
*Judith
Esther
*I Maccabees
*II Maccabees
*III Maccabees
*IV Maccabees
Job
Psalms
*Odes

Proverbs
Ecclesiastes
*Wisdom of Solomon
*Wisdom of Sirach
*Psalms of Solomon
Isaiah
Jeremiah
Lamentations
*Baruch
*Letter of Jeremiah
Ezekiel
Daniel
*Susanna
*Bel and the Snake
Hosea
Joel
Amos
Obadiah
Jonah
Micah
Nahum
Habakkuk
Zephaniah
Haggai
Zechariah
Malachi

*These are the apocryphal, or deutero-canonical, books that are not included in the Hebrew Scriptures or in the Bibles of most Protestant churches. They are included in the Bibles of the Eastern Orthodox and Roman Catholic churches, but the Catholic canon excludes I Esdras, III and IV Maccabees, Odes, and Psalms of Solomon. Some Bibles used by Orthodox Christians omit IV Maccabees, Odes, and Psalms of Solomon.

community of Babylonia from centuries earlier than that. Many of the Aramaic translations paraphrase rather than translate literally and often supplement with legendary and interpretive embellishments. The Aramaic version of the Hebrew Bible, called *Targum* ("translation"), is of great value to modern scholars and is studied to this day in traditional Jewish circles.

Commentaries

The traditional Jewish attitude toward the Hebrew Bible is that it is the inspired word of God, but Judaism does not adopt the approach of some forms of Christianity and insist that the literal meaning of the text must always be accepted. For over 2,000 years Judaism has developed a tradition of *interpreting* the Scriptures, accepting the literal meaning in most instances, but adopting an alternative understanding in others. Four modes of interpretation have been utilized since ancient times: the simple or surface meaning; homiletical explication (so as to derive a lesson from the text); allegory; and the explication of "secret" meaning. Allegory is used rather sparingly, and the "secret" interpretation is restricted largely to mystical works (see p. 106). The commentaries on the Bible that Jewish scholars have prepared over the centuries seek for the most part to expound the surface meaning of the text, along with homiletical interpretation. In traditional Jewish academies the Scriptures are studied to this day in conjunction with the Aramaic Targums and the commentaries of a number of medieval scholars written in Hebrew.

The most famous and widely quoted biblical commentary is that of Rashi (Rabbi Solomon Isaac), who lived during the eleventh century A.D. in France and the Rhineland. In Orthodox schools children are introduced to the study of the Torah with Rashi as soon as they are able to read and comprehend some Hebrew. People who grow up with this type of education retain for life an appreciation of Torah as refracted through the prism of Rashi's understanding, which emphasizes the rational and uncomplicated meaning of the biblical text.

Rashi begins his commentary to Genesis with these words:

> Said Rabbi Isaac, (God) could logically have begun the Torah with the verse "this month shall be the first of the months to you" (Exodus 12:2) for this was the first commandment given to Israel, and the essence of the Torah is its commandments. So why did He begin with the Creation? Because "the might of his deeds He related to his people, to give them the heritage of nations" (Psalm 111:6). If the nations of the world were to say to Israel, "You are robbers, for you conquered the lands of the seven nations (of Canaan)," they can retort: "All the land belongs to the Holy One, blessed be He. He created it and gave it to whomever it was proper in his eyes. By his will He gave it to them, and by his will he took it from them and gave it to us."

Here is Rashi on Genesis 28:10 (concerning Jacob's departure from Beersheba to go to Haran):

> The text could have said merely "Jacob went to Haran." Why was it necessary to make mention of his departure? It was to teach that the departure of a righteous man from a place makes an impression, for during the time that the righteous is in a city, he is its glory, he its light, he its beauty. When he departs from there gone is its glory, gone its light, gone its beauty. Thus also is it said of Naomi and Ruth that "she departed from the place." (Ruth 1)

Exodus 21:24 reads, "An eye for an eye, a tooth for a tooth, a hand for a hand, a foot for a foot." Understood literally, this means that if one causes someone else to lose one of these bodily parts, accidentally or otherwise, he shall be punished by having a similar bodily part removed from himself. Rashi in his commentary transmits the tradition of how this passage has been understood in Jewish law from a very early time:

> He who blinds the eye of his fellow shall pay him the monetary value of his eye, determinable by how much his total value would be reduced if he were to sell his services in the marketplace. In like manner we understand the other clauses as well. As our rabbis have expounded in the Talmud, it does not mean literally the taking of a limb.

CHAPTER FOUR

The Development of Judaism

Greeks, Romans, Jews

The Jews who returned to Jerusalem from the exile in Babylon lived peaceably as a community within the Persian Empire under the leadership of the Temple priests. About 330 B.C., however, the empire was overthrown by the forces of Alexander of Macedon, known as Alexander the Great, and the course of world history, including the development of Judaism, was changed for all time. (Since the time of the great Macedonian king the name "Alexander" has been bestowed by many Jews upon their male children. This custom originated as a mark of honor and homage to the great ruler.)

Judea, like all the other societies of the Near East, thus became part of the hellenistic world. Hellenism is a fusion of the civilization developed in Greece with that of the Semitic peoples and those of Egypt and Persia. Hellenism included not only the "high culture" of the Greeks, found in the works of philosophers and dramatists, but also Greek forms of social organization and commercial activity. The Greek language became widely disseminated among the Jewish upper classes, including the priesthood, and for a long time Greek names were common among even pious Jews.

When the Roman Empire absorbed Judea, about 270 years after Alexander's conquest, the process of hellenization continued, for the Romans deliberately took over and promulgated the culture of the Greeks. Greek, rather than Latin, was the language of the entire eastern portion of the Roman Empire.

It has long been believed by many that there was an innate antagonism between "Judaism and Hellenism," or between "Athens and Jerusalem," but scholars are coming more and more to recognize that this was not the case. Jews rose up against their hellenistic rulers when they were oppressed politically or when the rulers sought to impose restrictions on the free exercise of Jewish religious life, but in general Jewish and hellenistic culture were quite complementary to each other. Large Jewish communities developed in the hellenistic cities outside Judea, populated by migrating people who sought a material prosperity that Judea could not provide. Alexandria in Egypt was one such city, and the Hebrew Scriptures were translated into Greek for the benefit of the community there. Before long, there were relatively few Jews in Alexandria who could understand Hebrew, and their worship services were conducted in Greek.

Not all scholars agree about the influence of Hellenism on religious life in Judea, but many have suggested that the book of Ecclesiastes, with its rationalistic philosophy of life, reflects a Greek way of thinking. Others claim that the rhetorical devices developed by the rabbis to derive new law from scriptural verses, such as the argument by analogy or the argument *a fortiori* ("if *a* then how much the moreso *b*"), originated with Greek and Roman rhetoricians. Some say that the hellenistic idea of "unwritten law"—customary law that is observed by a community but which does not exist in statute form—lies behind the teaching of the rabbis that the written Torah is accompanied by another one that has handed down laws and traditions by word of mouth since the time of Moses. Many see in the Passover Seder a Greek symposium or Roman banquet, since many of the foods that are eaten, the wine that is drunk, the reclining next to the table, and the lengthy elaboration of the story of the Exodus are not prescribed in the Bible but are identical to hellenistic and Roman practice.

Alexander the Great died a few short years after his conquest of Persia, and his empire was divided among the Macedonian generals who had served him. The dynasty of the Ptolemies took possession of Egypt (the last of this line was Cleopatra), and Judea was for a time subject to it. Syria was ruled by the Seleucid dynasty, and Judea came under its sway as well. Jerusalem developed as a major center of hellenistic culture and population, and several Jewish families, following the tradition of the Greeks, became wealthy international merchants. A number of plots and intrigues divided the supporters of the Seleucids and the supporters of the Ptolemies within Judea as well as in other provinces of the two empires. Bitter rivalries and jealousy, accompanied by a desire to acquire as much material wealth as possible, were widespread in hellenistic society, and the Jews were not immune.

Matters came to a head about 170 B.C. when the Seleucid king Antiochus IV deposed the high priest of the Temple and appointed another in his place in return for the payment of a bribe. Soon thereafter the king appointed yet another high priest, upon his paying an even larger gratuity. Many Jews, naturally enough, came to question the legitimacy of such a priesthood, and its supporters were restricted to the extreme hellenizers within the community. They established a gymnasium near the Temple, not a place solely for athletic exercises but an academy in which the entire regimen of Greek tradition would be taught to the young men of Jerusalem, including the sons of the priests, and the Greek form of dress would be introduced. The Seleucid king was dismayed by the opposition of such a large portion of the Jews, and he sent troops into the Temple to steal some of its treasures to help finance a military campaign against Egypt. He also set up pagan altars in the countryside and one within the precincts of the Temple itself. A revolt against the desecrations and the persecutions was initiated by the priestly family of the Hasmoneans, and they were able to defeat the forces of Antiochus IV in 165 B.C. and take possession of the Temple. (The Hasmoneans consisted originally of five brothers and their father, and they are often called the "Maccabees" because one of the brothers, Judah, bore the epithet *maccabee*, meaning "hammerer." The history of the revolt of the Hasmoneans is given in the books of Maccabees, contained in the Apocrypha of the Old Testament, and in the writings of the first-century historian Josephus. Prior to the Hasmoneans, others had sought to engage the forces of Antiochus IV but had refused to defend themselves when attacked by the king's forces on the Sabbath. The Hasmonean brothers, however, resolved to fight on the Sabbath if necessary, and thus became the instrument of salvation for the Jews.)

The violence and the cruelties inflicted by the soldiers of King Antiochus IV were responsible for a major development in the history of religious ideology. The Torah speaks quite frequently of the rewards and punishments that will be meted out by God. These are described in very earthly terms: The righteous will enjoy health, long life, many children, and fertile crops and flocks, while the wicked will be afflicted with disease, death, exile, and the like. In the days of the persecutions of Antiochus, however, the opposite was true: It was the righteous who suffered barbaric torture and death for the sake of their faithfulness to the covenant with God. Accordingly, the promises of the Torah had to be reinterpreted, and a belief in reward and punishment that would take place after death took hold among many Jews. The book of Daniel, written during the period of the persecutions, spoke of the resurrection of the dead at the end of days. Although, according to the age-old belief of all the Semite peoples, both righteous and wicked were equal in death, this book asserted that souls would be restored to bodies when history reaches its consummation and all would rise from their graves for the final judgment. The righteous would live forever in a perfected world, and the wicked would persist forever in a state of torment. Other visions of reward and punishment appear in some of the apocryphal books, picturing the souls of the righteous living in heaven in the presence of God while the souls of the wicked endure the fires of Hell (*Gehenna*). Both teachings, that of the resurrection of the dead at the end of days and that of the eternal life of the soul after death, became part of Judaism—as well as Christianity and Islam—and thus the ideal of a just God was promulgated.

new
Theodicy

The Hasmonean rededication of the Temple is celebrated to this day in the Jewish festival of Hanukka. The Hasmoneans established this festival as an eight-day period of rejoicing on the analogy of the eight-day Feast of Tabernacles when, according to the book of Kings, Solomon's Temple had been dedicated. The Hasmoneans established an independent Judean state, reserving for themselves both the high priestly role and, eventually, the title of king as well. They struck coins, recovered by archeologists, with the inscription "priest to God Most High," which indicates that they considered themselves to be the successors to Melkizedek, the pre-Israelite priest-king of Jerusalem in the days of Abraham, who had combined the two offices in his own person. They established an alliance with Rome, providing that each would come to the aid of the other in time of need, and thereby served notice upon the Seleucids that any attempt to reabsorb Judea would be very costly. One of the later Hasmonean kings conquered the Edomites (traditionally the descendants of Esau, Jacob's brother) and forcibly converted them to Judaism. This same king destroyed the Samaritan Temple in Shechem.

Ironically, although the Hasmoneans had assumed power as representatives of a purified Judaism, loyal to the responsibilities imposed by the sacred covenant with God, the dynasty came to be identified with cruelty and oppression. Even within the family itself, one hatched plots against another as each sought power. Sects and parties arose among the Jews, many of whom questioned the legitimacy of Hasmonean rule. At first the Hasmonean right to the high priesthood was questioned as, though they were a priestly family, theirs was not the line from which the former high priests had come. Later, some insisted that the Hasmoneans did not deserve the kingship, since it was only from the family of David that the true kings of the Jews could come. Messianic hopes and revolutionary expectations arose among the Jews opposed to Hasmonean rule, and texts written in a kind of code began to be circulated among those who awaited the dawning of a new order. These texts never referred to the rulers by name, and their authorship was disguised as well. They are called "pseudepigrapha" by modern scholars, a term signifying that these writings were attributed to ancient sages or patriarchs who could not possibly have written them. Among them were texts attributed to Enoch and the twelve sons of Jacob. Pseudepigrapha continued to be written into the second century A.D. and played an important role in the apocalyptic ideologies, or the visions of the end of the world, that developed among some Jews.

During one dispute within the Hasmonean family about the royal succession, the mediation of Rome was requested. Rome, after all, was a fraternal ally of Judea, linked by treaty for a century. The Romans, however, could see that there was no further viability in the Hasmonean dynasty and chose instead to absorb Judea into their empire in 63 B.C. Some years thereafter they appointed Herod, the grandson of one of the Edomite converts to Judaism, as king of the Jews. He sought to obtain legitimacy in the eyes of the people through marriage to a daughter of the Hasmoneans, but his cruelty to the members of his own family, as well as to any and all who opposed him among the people at large, made it impossible for Herod to win any degree of affection or loyalty. (As an able administrator, there were of course many who depended upon him for patronage and position, so in spite of the fact that he was widely despised, Herod reigned for nearly forty years.) He was responsible for a number of building projects, the most famous of which was the complete reconstruction of the Temple of Jerusalem.

Herod's Temple was said to be one of the most magnificent buildings in the ancient world.

Upon Herod's death, the territory of the Jews was divided among several Roman appointees for administrative purposes. Jerusalem and its environs was usually under a procurator, an official sent directly from Rome. There was an attempt to satisfy Jewish religious sensibilities, as provided in Roman law, and some of the procurators were decent and honest men. Others, however, were cruel and rapacious, demanding ever-increasing payments in money, grain, and animals from the peasantry. (In addition to the taxation demanded by Rome, Jews also had to pay the tithes ordained in the Torah for the support of the Temple priesthood and the communal sacrifices.) Even if Rome itself did not demand more than the people could afford, the system of tax collection lent itself to extortion and injustice. Tax collectors were assigned particular districts, from which they were expected to raise stipulated amounts for the government. They could, however, use any means they wished to raise this money (tolls were commonly assessed on roads), and whatever they raised in excess of that amount was theirs to keep. There was always temptation to make the exactions upon the people as large as possible. An honest and fair tax collector was such a rarity that the religious tradition often spoke of "tax collectors" and "sinners" as synonymous.

Peasant revolts against the government occurred under both Herod and the procurators. These revolts were fueled by the people's desire to escape taxation as well as their messianic expectations—the conviction that the time was at hand when God would send his chosen king of the house of David to destroy not only the wicked government of Rome, but also Jews of wealth and social position and the corrupt priests of the Temple. Many of these rebels preached what would today be called a form of communism, claiming that all private property is a sin against God. The great revolt against Rome broke out in 66 A.D. in Galilee, spreading to Jerusalem, where the rebels seized control of the city and the Temple. There they murdered many of the chief priests and others in the wealthier classes and destroyed the records of debt that were kept in the city. Rome was forced to gather a large force to combat the rebels, and the city was placed under siege. It was not until the year 70 A.D. that the city fell and the Temple was destroyed by fire. Thousands of Jews were killed, both by the Roman forces and by the rebels themselves; others were sent into slavery to distant parts of the empire.

All was not lost, however. Not all Jews expected a messianic liberator to appear, and not all Jews looked upon the destruction of the Temple as the ultimate tragedy. One rabbi likened it to the felling of a great wall that separated Israel from his Father in heaven. Another comforted a disciple, who had wept upon seeing the ruins of the Temple, "the place where the sins of Israel were atoned," by saying: "My son, do not grieve. We have another atonement that is as effective as this. It is acts of mercy, for scripture says 'I desire mercy and not sacrifice' " (Abot de Rabbi Natan lla)

The Jewish Sects

Sadducees, Essenes, Christians, Pharisees

During the hellenistic and Roman eras there seem to have been three major sects within the Jewish people—the Sadduces, Essenes and Pharisees. It should be noted, however, that the majority of Jews were not "card-carrying members" of any particular sect. Most Jews lived by the laws of the Torah and followed the instructions given by the religious authorities, but they may not have been too punctilious about all of the rules of tithing or about the ritual purifications that the various sects advocated. The sects seem to have been organized on the order of fraternal brotherhoods, the members of which were devoted to a particular discipline and interpretation of religious law. The leaders of the sects were scholars known as Scribes or, at a later date, rabbis, who often pursued worldly occupations in addition to their responsibilities as religious teachers. According to the historian Josephus, the majority of the people inclined toward the teachings of the Pharisees.

The Sadducees are so named because they adhered to the primacy of the Sadokites, the descendants of Sadok, who was Solomon's high priest. They were the guardians of "old-time religion," teaching that only the written law of the Torah constituted the revelation of God. They interpreted this written law literally, although they accepted a few modifications of practice if they could be justified by a text from the Torah. They refused to accept the belief in the resurrection of the dead or the survival of the soul, holding instead that God's rewards and punishments are distributed during earthly life. They believed that people make their choices according to their own free will and that the pleasures and pains that God allots to individuals are always just. They also differed with other Jewish sects about the dates of certain holidays. Since the Sadducees were for the most part Temple priests and wealthy aristocrats, their influence over the people as a whole was rather limited, and during much of their existence they had to abide by the rulings and interpretations of the Pharisees. (This extended even to the procedures of the Temple sacrifices, although the chief priests were themselves Sadducees.) With the destruction of the Temple the Sadducees ceased to exist as a sect.

The Essenes, too, believed in the primacy of the descendants of Sadok, but they rejected the priests of the Temple as impure and saw as the true sons of Sadok only those priests who had attached themselves to their own brotherhood. Josephus states that during the first century there were about 4,000 Essenes settled in various cities. They lived together in separate communities, most of which were celibate and monastic in organization. Since they did not have children of their own, they adopted the children of other people and raised them according to their beliefs. Men joining the Essene orders gave all their personal property to the group and renounced the possession of anything that was not necessary for a modest and simple style of life.

They engaged in agricultural pursuits and always dressed in white. In recent decades the remains of the Essene settlement at Qumran, near the Dead Sea, have been discovered, as well as a large library of texts that were hidden away in caves by the people of the settlement. These are the Dead Sea Scrolls, including biblical texts and commentaries, the rules of discipline of the order, religious poetry, and their vision of the end of days.

The Essenes believed that whatever occurs, including the choices that humans make, is the result of the will of God. They believed in the immortality of the soul. Souls, they said, emanate from the finest ether and become entangled "in the prison-house of the body, to which they are dragged down by a sort of natural spell; but when they are released from the bonds of the flesh, then, as though liberated from a long servitude, they rejoice and are borne aloft" (Josephus, *Jewish War* 2:155). They had a reputation as accurate foretellers of the future and as masters of the art of healing. Except for the oaths required when one joined the order, they would not take oaths; other Jews, even the violent King Herod, were convinced that they always spoke the truth, so no oath was asked of them. They frequently immersed themselves in water as a means of spiritual purification (baptism). From the Dead Sea Scrolls we learn that they followed a calendar that was quite different from that of other Jewish sects; it included a number of additional sacred days. They anticipated a great war between the "sons of light" and the "sons of darkness," following which a new Temple would be built in Jerusalem, replacing the old, impure one. At the end of days, the Prophet and the "Messiahs of Aaron and Israel" would appear. The Messiah of Israel would be of the line of David, while the Messiah of Aaron is the priestly ruler. Quite possibly they identified this Priestly Messiah with the "Teacher of Righteousness," the founder of their own order who would return from heaven.

The Christians, of course, originated as a Jewish sect in the first century A.D., the followers of Jesus of Nazareth.

(Christians are called "Nazarenes" in Jewish texts.) Jesus preached the imminent coming of the Kingdom of God, when the present order of existence would end and a new heaven and a new earth would appear. All wickedness would be destroyed, with the dead resurrected for judgment and the righteous living forever in God's Kingdom. His ministry was primarily to the poor, "the lost sheep of the house of Israel," and he taught that the wealthy would have to give all that they had to the poor if they were to be worthy of the Kingdom. He seems to have shared many teachings with the Essenes: the disdain for wealth, a prohibition of divorce, a prohibition of oaths, a disdain for petitional prayer (the Essenes recited prayers of praise and thanksgiving, but they seem not to have offered petitions or requests to God, believing, like Jesus, that God knows the needs of humans without their having to remind Him of them). Jesus probably regarded himself—and was looked upon by his followers during his lifetime—as the Prophet of the Kingdom. At his death his followers came to believe that he had fulfilled the destiny of the Messiah of the line of David and styled him "the Christ," the anointed one (the Greek equivalent of "messiah"). Those who believed that he had risen from the dead also expected his return from heaven as the ruler of the new age, the Priestly Messiah of the Essenes. Christianity ceased to be a Jewish sect when the early Church, at the urging of Paul, opened its ranks to non-Jews without requiring them to accept the ritual prescriptions of the Torah (primarily circumcision, observance of the Sabbath, and dietary restrictions). The Church thus became a group that was not governed by Jewish law, nor did it retain a predominantly Jewish membership in an ethnic sense.

Many people over the centuries (Christians, Muslims, even many Jews) have wondered why the Jewish people as a whole did not accept Jesus as their King Messiah. First, it should be noted that the synoptic gospels (Matthew, Mark, and Luke) indicate quite clearly that Jesus did not go about among the people of his day proclaiming himself the Messiah. He never asked anyone to follow him because he was their King. It was only after his death that the associates of Jesus publicly affirmed that he had been the King Messiah, and that he had died in fulfillment of Scripture (I Corinthians 15:3). While some Jewish sectarians believed that it was the destiny of the expected king to die, the great mass of the people had no such expectation, nor would it have made any sense to them. Those Jews of the first century who believed in the coming of a messianic king awaited him because he would, they thought, initiate a mighty Kingdom of Israel to whom Rome and Persia and the other principalities of the day would pay tribute. They did not expect the coming of a king who would never reign, who would instead be put to death. This is why so few Jews heeded the call of the first Christians.

The Pharisees were the sect from which all the later forms of Judaism developed. They of course accepted the revealed character of the written Torah, but they also believed that an "oral Torah"—one that does not exist in writing but has instead been transmitted by word of mouth from each generation of sages to another—was also revealed to Moses. This oral Torah consists of various laws and observances, as well as methods of interpreting the written Torah so as to derive new legislation from it. Especially after the Hebrew Scriptures had been translated into Greek, making them available to the entire literate world of the time, the sages of the Pharisees came to look upon the oral Torah as the special possession of the Jewish people and upon themselves as the only legitimate interpreters of the law. (The name *Pharisees* may mean "separatists"; that is, those who separate themselves from people who do not properly observe the ritual law; or it may mean "interpreters," those who interpret and develop the law.) The sages of the Pharisees took upon themselves the obligation to "raise up many disciples," and they sought whenever possible to educate scholars of the law among the children of the poor.

The people who inclined toward the Pharisees seem to have been what we would call "the middle class"—city dwellers and those peasant farmers who had risen above the so-called "people of the land," the very poor. They placed a great value upon learning and debating the fine points of the law. They believed that while God controls all things, free will is still granted to humanity. (The Talmud preserves two statements of Pharisaic sages on this subject: "All is foreseen, yet permissiveness is given," and "All is in the hands of Heaven except for the fear of Heaven.") They believed in the resurrection of the dead and the reward of everlasting life that would be the lot of the righteous. Most of them accepted the popular hope for the coming of a Messiah, a king from the line of David who would be both a mighty warrior and a compassionate sage. Some of the scholars, however, did not expect a Messiah, maintaining like many modern scholars that the messianic references in the Hebrew Scriptures were meant to apply to kings of ancient Judah.

The Pharisees through their interpretive tradition were able to make the Torah applicable to new social challenges as they arose. In effect, they wrested the teaching and application of the Torah out of the hands of the Temple priesthood, most of whom were Sadducees who did not accept the concept of a developing system of law. Because this interpretive tradition was well developed by the time of the Temple's destruction in the great revolt, Judaism was able to survive. Since the largest portion of the people looked to the Pharisaic sages for guidance, the end of the sacrificial system in the Jerusalem temple could be accepted, for the Pharisees mandated other forms of religious expression that could take its place.

Shortly before the final conflagration in Jerusalem, Rabbi Johanan son of Zakkai was smuggled outside the walls of the city (where the population was being held captive by the leaders of the rebellion) and made his way to the camp of the Roman commander. He asked permission to set up an academy of study in the town of Jabneh. This permission was granted. Rabbi Johanan's academy was subsequently recognized by the Roman authorities as the Jewish institution of self-government and was allowed certain powers over the community. In effect, it was the continuation of the Jewish high court that had exercised jurisdiction prior to the revolt, except that now it was a purely Pharisaic institution rather than one composed of both Pharisees and Sadducees, including the high priest, as it had been before. The court functioned in both a legislative and judicial capacity and had authority over both religious and certain civil matters. (Jewish law as such makes no distinction between these two categories.) Within the academy there were often two points of view that would become apparent when specific matters were discussed, one a more liberal attitude and the second a stricter one. Two methodologies of interpreting the Scriptures also became apparent. One held that "the Torah speaks the language of human beings," meaning that interpretations of Scripture should not be forced because its words are meant to be taken in their normal, everyday sense. The other held that each letter and syllable of the Torah was meant to convey a lesson, so in addition to accepting Scripture's normal, everyday sense, it was legitimate to intuit extremely fine nuances from it, even from a single word or letter. When the rabbis of the academy had to pronounce a decision on a matter that had come before them, they were governed by majority vote.

The early tradition of the Pharisees had held that, while the written Torah was meant to be transmitted in written form, the oral Torah was not to be put in writing. The teachings of the sages were to be memorized, rather, and transmitted by word of mouth from scholar to scholar. It did not take long, of course, for the number of interpretations and decisions that constituted the oral Torah to become so vast that even the most brilliant scholars would have trouble recalling all of them (they also had to remember the names of the various sages who had originated or transmitted a decision). For this reason the head of the academy in the early years of the third century, Rabbi Judah the Nasi ("prince" or "patriarch"), resolved to reduce the oral Torah to writing. He collected the various decisions and interpretations that were known to the rabbis of the academy, including the private written notes that some of them had made for themselves. Then, in about 220 A.D., he introduced the first authoritative summary of the rabbinic traditon to that date. This was the *Mishna* ("repetition"). The Mishna, based upon the laws of the Hebrew Bible, is the source of all subsequent Jewish law to the present day and is an object of study in the academies of all the forms of Judaism.

During the two centuries following the promulgation of the Mishna, the rabbis continued to discuss and refine the laws of the Mishna. These discussions, printed together with the text of the Mishna itself, constitute the Palestinian (or Jerusalem) Talmud. The word *talmud* means "learning." The Palestinian Talmud remains an object of study in the more advanced Jewish academies.

The Synagogue

The synagogue is the invention of Pharisaic Judaism, and it is the institution through which the faith was preserved following the destruction of the Temple. The Greek term *synagogue* is a translation of the Hebrew *bet keneset*, "house of assembly," and implies that it was the place where the men of the community gathered on public occasions. Other terms for the synagogue that describe its function in the community are "house of prayer" and "house of study."

The synagogue came into being while the Temple still stood. The Pharisees believed that priests and Levites who represented the various Judean communities should be present at the public sacrifices in the Temple every morning and evening, observing the actions of the Temple priests who offered up the sacrifices on behalf of the entire nation. The Torah prescribed that Jewish males over twenty years of age were obliged to bring animal offerings to the Temple at the three festivals of Passover, Pentecost, and Tabernacles, but people were not obligated to visit the Temple at any other time unless they had personal offerings to bring (for the expiation of certain sins, the presentation of first-born animals, the offering of birds by a woman after the birth of a child, and so on). Accordingly, it was arranged that men of a particular district would be divided into various "courses," or groups, each course to include priests, Levites, and ordinary Jews. It was the obligation of the priests and Levites in each course to go up to Jerusalem to observe the sacrifices during a specified period of time. While they were at the Temple, the ordinary Jews who were attached to that course would gather together in their own town to read the Scriptures and recite prayers. It was in this way that the worship services of the synagogue originated. The prayer services corresponded to the public sacrifices that were being offered at the Temple at the same time— *shaharit* at dawn and *minha* near dusk. Subsequently rabbinic authorities added the third service, the *maarib*, later in the evening, to correspond to the burning of animal parts that had taken place on the Temple altar at that time. After the Temple had been destroyed, these three prayer services continued as a replacement for the offerings of the Temple.

The liturgy that developed in the synagogues was at first loosely structured. As time went on, the rabbinical leaders established a form of prayer that became standardized. The reading of a section of the Torah was part of every Sabbath morning service, along with a shorter selection from the Torah on Monday and Thursday mornings (the customary market days when more people came to the service). In Palestine for a time the custom was to read the entire Torah over a three-year period, but in the synagogues of Babylonia the Torah was completed in one year. This requires lections, or readings, of about six chapters for each Sabbath, which is still the practice in Orthodox and most Conservative synagogues throughout the world.

The text of the Torah is chanted, according to a traditional mode. In ancient times it was accompanied by its Aramaic translation. Several readers are called up to read sections from the Torah, or at least to recite the blessings for the reading if their Hebrew is not fluent enough for them to recite the text itself. The reader of the first section is always a priest (*kohen*) in Orthodox and Conservative synagogues; the reader of the second section is always a Levite; only thereafter are ordinary Jews (*yisrael*) called up for the reading. The custom developed early on to read a chapter or so from one of the books of the Prophets following the lection from the Torah; this is still done in synagogues throughout the world. Mishna Megilla 4:3 stipulates that a quorum *(minyan)* of ten men is required before public worship can begin or the Torah be read. This is still the rule in Orthodoxy. Non-Orthodox groups are often willing to count women as part of the minyan, and in Reform Judaism public worship without a minyan may sometimes occur.

Synagogues may be housed in grandiose structures, or they may function in a single room in an undistinguished building. In fact, worship services may take place anywhere; a minyan of Jews may gather either indoors or outdoors to pray together, and the service is as consecrated as any held in the most elaborate structure. There are a few features, though, that are common to practically all permanent synagogue spaces. The Holy Ark, in which the scrolls of the Torah are kept, is ordinarily set in the wall in the direction facing Jerusalem. Modern scrolls, like those used thousands of years ago, are handwritten on parchment in Hebrew characters without any punctuation marks. The spacing of the lines is dictated by traditional regulations going back thousands of years. A synagogue may have one or more scrolls, but each one contains the complete text of the Torah, from Genesis through Deuteronomy. The parchment is attached at either end to wooden rollers, called the "tree of life." Above the Ark is an Eternal Light. On either side of the Ark there is often a seven-branched candelabrum, derived from the golden candelabrum that was kept perpetually lit in the Temple of Jerusalem. In Orthodox synagogues, however, the candelabrum either would not have seven branches or, if it did, one of its branches would be unlit, since it is considered improper to reproduce in exact detail the appurtenance that stood in the Temple. The leader of the service stands behind a reading desk that faces the

Ark. Any Jew who knows the ritual is qualified to lead the service, although larger synagogues often engage a cantor (*hazzan*) trained in the music of the liturgy. Whether layman or trained professional, the prayer leader represents the congregation as he brings its praises and petitions before God. At times the congregation prays in silence and at other times audibly, but it also expresses its devotion and its unity with the prayer leader by responding to his words, at the appropriate times, with the vocable hallowed by thousands of years—*amen* ("it is true and sure").

The Jewish Diaspora

Jews had been settled in many cities in the hellenistic and Roman territories, and in the city of Rome itself, for centuries prior to the revolt against Roman rule, and these communities were augmented by people who left Judea and Galilee after the revolt. Synagogues had been established in these cities, and they also existed in the large Jewish settlement in Babylonia that dated back to the time of Jeremiah. There was, in fact, continuous traffic between Judea and Babylonia. Scholars came from Babylonia to study with the rabbinic authorities in Galilee (where the academy was located, since the Romans did not want it in Jerusalem). After ordination, these scholars returned to Babylonia where they established centers of Jewish learning. The scholars of the academies in Babylonia soon came to rival those in Palestine both in numbers and in their mastery of the law. The Mishna was the text that they discussed and, like their colleagues in Palestine, they, too, produced a Talmud. The Babylonian Talmud is a far vaster collection of materials than the Palestinian. It includes the text of the Mishna, the discussions of the rabbis of Babylonia, and countless citations from Palestinian rabbis as well. The Babylonian Talmud is the major text studied in rabbinic academies to this day anywhere in the world. Thus, when a Jew refers to "the Talmud," he means the one produced in Babylonia, concluded about the year 500 A.D. It is referred to as "the sea of the Talmud," and every Jew who is capable of doing so is urged to "search in it, and search in it again, for everything is contained in it" (Abot 5:22). Not only rabbis but all Jews who have a love for their tradition are expected, to the extent that they are able, to study the Talmud.

The heads of the academies in Babylonia were involved in the government of the Jews there, in conjunction with the political leader recognized by the Persian government as ruler of the Jews. His title was "head of the exile," a hereditary position restricted to a specific family claiming descent from David. When the Muslim Arabs overthrew the Persians and conquered Babylonia in the seventh century A.D., they permitted the autonomous government of the Jewish community to continue. An internal revolt had to be dealt with, however, during the eighth century. This was the movement of the Karaites, a sect that wished to overthrow the Talmud and the entire structure of rabbinic Judaism, retaining only the Bible. It made considerable headway for a few centuries, particularly among the poor and some disgruntled intellectuals, but it fell into decline because it eventually became apparent that biblical law itself, without development or interpretation, could not be applied to contemporary situations. The Karaites rejected the rabbinic traditions and interpretations, but they were forced to develop their own, which, in many instances, amounted to a reclamation of what the rabbis had instituted originally. Karaism did inspire Jewish scholars to reexamine the text of the Hebrew Bible very carefully, stimulating a detailed analysis of its grammar and syntax. Influenced by the example of Islam, both Karaism and rabbinic Judaism began to take an interest in metaphysical philosophy, particularly the analysis of the attributes of God. A very small number of Karaites still exist scattered over the world, but they maintain no organized relationship with other Jews.

Just as the Jews of Palestine suffered a decline due to economic conditions and oppressive laws imposed by the Christians of the Byzantine Empire, so, too, did the Jews of

Babylonia undergo a decline as a result of Islamic persecutions. Jews always remained in both ancient lands, but they ceased to form centers of cultural creativity. The influence of the Babylonian academies lived on, however, in a new land which became a major center of Jewish settlement, Spain. Jews were probably present in Roman Spain by the third century, and thereafter their number grew. The Catholic Church, locked in a struggle with other forms of early Christianity, instituted various types of anti-Jewish legislation, so it is not surprising that when the Muslim Arabs, invading from Morocco, took over much of Spain, the Jews welcomed them. Although there were periods when Muslim extremists held sway and Jews (as well as Christians) were subject to religious persecution and civic restrictions, during much of the period of Muslim control the Jews prospered and flourished. Scholars were imported from Babylonia, and they gave direction and vigor to the development of both Jewish religion and secular culture. The Jews of Spain adopted the Arabic language, which is the tongue in which the Jewish philosophers, disciples of Plato or Aristotle, wrote their works. (Jewish biblical commentaries and poetry, even if it dealt with secular themes, were ordinarily written in Hebrew.) There were Jews in high positions of government under the Muslims, others who were scientists and physicians, and others who were international merchants or administrators of large estates. The flowering of Jewish cultural life in Muslim Spain is one of the high points in the vast sweep of Jewish history.

The peaceful and prosperous lot of the Jews in Spain was not destined to last, however. As Christian princes pushed the Muslim rulers out of the country, the lot of the Jews more often than not became a sad one. Church preachers inflamed the populace against the Jews, and many communities were completely destroyed, the inhabitants butchered by mobs. Often the Jews were given the choice of baptism or death, and a considerable number chose baptism. They were known as "new Christians," and it was not long before many in the populace became envious of the success and good fortune of these "new Christians," just as formerly they had resented the position of the Jews. "New Christians" were accused of being *marranos*, a term of abuse meaning one who outwardly feigns Christianity but in secret observes the rites of Judaism. (There were no doubt some true "marranos" among those who had been forced to accept baptism in order to save their lives, but an even larger number of converts were people who, sincerely desiring to become part of the Church community, had been abused and rejected for their efforts and, as a consequence, had reverted to Jewish beliefs and practices.) The Inquisition, the office of the Church whose duty it was to root out heresy, was set upon those "new Christians" who had been accused of "judaizing tendencies." People found it quite easy to accuse anyone whom they disliked of this "crime."

By the late fifteenth century the Church decided that a major reason for the continuing attraction of Judaism to the "new Christians" was the fact that Jews as a group still remained in Spain. Many of these people were relatives or friends of Christians and so, the reasoning went, if the Jews were no longer around, the Christians might become better Christians. Accordingly, a decree was promulgated expelling all Jews from Spain in 1492. According to some historians, the expulsion of these thousands of people, as well as the work of the Inquisition in persecuting those who remained behind within the Church, contributed to the subsequent decline of Spain as a major world power.

For the Spanish Jews the expulsion from the homeland where they had lived for centuries was a tragedy of the same magnitude as the destruction of Jerusalem some 1,400 years before. The expulsion, however, initiated the dispersion of the Sephardic Jews from Spain and Portugal (*Sepharad* in Hebrew) throughout the Mediterranean world, and the great gifts that many of them possessed came in this way to enrich other societies and Jewish communities in whose midst they settled. The Sultan of Turkey invited the Sephardic Jews to his land, and a number of them rose to great prominence there. Others went to Italy and Holland. The first Jewish settlers in North America came to New Amsterdam in 1654; these were people from the Sephardic dispersion. Wherever they went, they took with them their love of poetry, song and learning, which included not only the study of the Torah and Talmud and the commentaries upon these texts, but also the study of philosophy and the sciences. The language that they brought with them, in addition to Hebrew, is called Ladino, an old form of Spanish that is often written in the characters of the Hebrew alphabet.

Besides the large Jewish settlement in Spain, there were Jews who made their home in countries of northern Europe from a very early period. Jews settled in England, but the community as a whole was expelled at the end of the thirteenth century, not to return (except for a few who lived there *incognito*) until the government of Cromwell in the 1660s. Jews lived in many parts of France; an expulsion took place from Paris and its environs early in the thirteenth century because many of the nobility and prelates of the Church were deeply in debt to Jews. By arranging their expulsion, the debtors no longer had to repay their debts. Jews had been living in Germany before the ancestors of many of the "Germans"; they had settled in the Rhineland during the days of the Roman Empire. This was no protection, however, from persecution and religious fanaticism. Thousands were slaughtered by the armies of the Crusaders who made their way across Europe on their way to battle Islam in the Holy Land. The lot of the Jews in the various German states varied from time to time and from place to place. Many of the poorer people came to hate the Jews because they had to go to them for loans of money, paying interest and leaving their personal property as pledges. Christians were forbidden by Church law during much of the Middle Ages to charge interest, so it fell to the Jews to discharge this necessary economic function. (Jews were forbidden to own land and could not belong to the guilds of artisans, so many were forced into money-lending for a livelihood.) When disturbances threatening the Jews broke out in one German city, they often could find refuge in another. For a time they and their property were considered the possession of the Holy Roman Emperor, who was the nominal sovereign over the various German states. In theory this protected them from being persecuted by local rulers and nobles, but in actuality the emperor's powers were quite limited and the Jews were at the mercy of those who wished to take advantage of them.

At various times and in various places Jews were forced to wear distinctive clothing. In many cities they were confined to a specific district (the term *ghetto* comes from Venice, where the Jewish district was in the area of the iron foundry, the *ghetto*). Perhaps the most horrifying experience that Jews had to undergo during the Middle Ages, and one that continued into the modern era, was the periodic outbreaks of violence and murder that accompanied the "blood libel"—the allegation that Jews would kidnap and murder a non-Jew to obtain his blood for the Passover ritual. The blood libel first appeared in Spain during the persecutions there, but it made its way to all the countries of Europe. It was denounced by the Papacy, but many of the common people clung tenaciously to it. It probably originated as a result of the emphasis in Church teaching that the bread and wine of the Eucharist actually become the body and blood of Christ, which is then consumed by the worshipper. Since the Eucharist, according to the Church, is derived from the Jewish Passover meal, ignorant and bigoted people could easily become convinced that blood played a role in the Jewish observance, too.

Beginning in the eleventh century there was a large movement of Jews from Germany into Poland. Several of the Polish kings warmly welcomed the Jews into their domain and appointed a number of them as administrators of their estates. Jews were allowed considerable autonomy, and a vigorous cultural and religious life flourished among them. The language that they brought with them from Germany was Yiddish ("Jewish"), which consists of a basically German vocabulary with an admixture of Hebrew. It is written in Hebrew alphabetic characters. Yiddish was the language of everyday discourse within the Jewish community of Poland, while Hebrew remained the language of prayer and religious scholarship. A rich literature developed in Yiddish, and the language continues to play an important role among East European Jews who have settled in North America, Argentina, and elsewhere in the world. It is part of the heritage of Ashkenazic Jews (those whose ancestry is traceable to Germany or Eastern Europe), just as Ladino is part of the heritage of the Sephardic Jews.

Although a number of the Polish kings were warmly disposed toward the Jews, there was a great deal of religious prejudice against them among the peasantry. Hatred of Jews was also fanned by the position that some Jews held as representatives of, or intermediaries for, the nobility in its relations with the peasantry. Hatred of Jews was particularly strong among the Ukrainian peasants of eastern Poland. In 1648 they revolted against their Polish overlords and, in the course of the rebellion, over 100,000 Jews were slaughtered. From that time on, the position of Jews in Poland was not what it had been before. The majority of them lived in poverty, particularly after the destruction of the Polish kingdom and the occupation of the major areas where Jews lived by the Russian Empire. Under Russian rule, the persecution of the Jews became a matter of public policy. Jews were restricted to certain areas of the country (the "Pale of Settlement") and only a small number were allowed higher secular education. There was even a period when Jewish children could be forcibly taken from their parents and conscripted for a twenty-five-year term of service in the Russian army. One Russian official commented that the aim of the country's policy toward the Jews was to convert one-third to Christianity, encourage one-third to emigrate, and leave one-third to starve. The term "pogrom" comes from Russia; it means a riot organized for the specific purpose of slaughtering Jews and looting their property.

A large number of Jews did fulfill the Russian official's hope by emigrating to the United States. There was a small Sephardic settlement there during the colonial period and the early part of the nineteenth century. A larger number of German Jews came during the middle part of the century as part of the general immigration to the United States of people from Germany and Central Europe. A veritable flood of Jews came to America, however, from Russia and Poland during the latter part of the nineteenth century and the first decades of the twentieth. Their numbers overwhelmed the previous waves of Jewish immigration, so that today when one speaks of "Jewish culture" in America he often means a specifically East European heritage in the form of foods, Yiddish language, and humor. The Jews came to find freedom in this country and, like other immigrants, they were able to find it. This is because the United States of America is the first country that did not make religion or ethnicity a condition of citizenship and that made all its citizens technically equal before the law.

The settlement of Jews in the Western Hemisphere completed their dispersion over the entire globe. In ancient times there was an extensive Jewish population in Yemen; most of these people have settled in the State of Israel. There was also a large number of black Jews in Ethiopia, although poverty and disease and persecution have decimated them. (During the last years of the twentieth century, the remnant of the Ethiopian Jews is in the process of coming to Israel.) India, too, had several Jewish groups, some of whom are physically indistinguishable from their Hindu neighbors. A large number of these people have also come to Israel. In the mid-nineteenth century a community of Jews was discovered in China, in appearance indistinguishable from the other Chinese of their province. Their origin seems to stem from a group of Persian Jews who went to China to trade and intermarried with the Chinese. By the time of the community's discovery, though, it had dwindled to a very small number and by now its people are fully merged into the surrounding Chinese Muslim population.

It would be wrong to think of Jewish life during the Middle Ages, as well as Jewish life in modern times in places like Russia and Poland, as a story of unalloyed persecution. There were times and places when Jews enjoyed themselves to the fullest, when relationships with their neighbors were cordial and warm. Besides, the world as a whole was for most people a squalid and brutal place. Christians and Muslims were as capable of murdering and torturing each other as they were of persecuting Jews. The vision of true human equality came closer to fulfillment in the United States (except, at first, for the slaves), but for most of the countries of Europe it did not become even a partial reality until the French Revolution and Napoleon. The French Revolution called for an end to all ethnic distinctions, seeking instead to build a society based on liberty, equality, and fraternity. In 1807 Napoleon convoked an assembly of rabbis and Jewish notables, who declared that in the new France every Jew was religiously bound to consider his non-Jewish fellow citizens as his brothers and sisters, to aid, protect, and love them in the same measures as if they were Jews, to consider the land of his birth or adoption as his fatherland and to love and defend it when called upon. Thus, for the first time, a secular society was born; each person was expected to participate, both emotionally and physically, in the civic and social life of the land, transcending any religious or ethnic loyalties he might have. The armies of Napoleon carried these ideals into Germany and Central Europe. Many Jews thought that the "days of the Messiah" had come, that all would be well forevermore.

Not all Christians, however, were willing to embrace the ideals of the Revolution and regard the Jews of their land as their brothers and sisters. Doctrines of romantic nationalism speaking of "blood and soil" took root in Central Europe, and even in France itself, as a reaction against the liberal and egalitarian ideals of the Revolution. Thus, "anti-Semitism" was born during the latter part of the nineteenth century. The world has always known "anti-Judaism"—ideas in opposition to the teachings of the religion of the Jews— but anti-Semitism was something else. Anti-Semitism originally meant not only opposition to the Jewish religion, but also the belief that there is something essentially evil in

Jewish blood and that Jews by their very presence act as a corrupting influence on the peoples and cultures of the lands in which they live. Even conversion to Christianity could not save the Jew from the enmity of the anti-Semite; the Holocaust, the attempted extermination of all the Jews of Europe during the Second World War, was the inevitable culmination of these teachings.

As mentioned earlier, the response of many Jews to anti-Semitism was Zionism, the movement initiated during the last years of the nineteenth century that insisted the only way in which Jews could escape persecution was through return to the ancient homeland— Zion, the land of Israel. The culmination of Zionism is the State of Israel, proclaimed May 14, 1948, risen out of the ashes of the Holocaust.

Judaism, Christianity, Islam

Over the centuries the vast majority of Jews in the world found themselves living in lands where the dominant religion was either Christianity or Islam. Christians often found it difficult to fathom why Jews refused to accept Christianity: After all, wasn't Jesus a Jew? Didn't the New Testament, which is based on the premise that Jesus was the Christ, the King Messiah of the Jews, flow directly out of the Hebrew Scriptures? What should be remembered, of course, is that Jews, except for those who have become Christians, do not accept the New Testament as inspired Scripture. In the same manner, neither Christianity nor Judaism regard the Koran, the sacred book of Islam, as Holy Scripture. Muslims believe that God Himself revealed the text of the Koran to Muhammad and that Muhammad, who established Islam during the first decades of the seventh century A.D., was the last and the greatest of the prophets, the fulfillment of both the Hebrew Scriptures and the New Testament. Neither Christianity nor Judaism incorporates these claims of Islam into its religious teaching; in like manner, Judaism does not incorporate the claims of the

New Testament. (Of course, if Christianity during the centuries of its existence had brought into being a world of peace and universal well-being, many more Jews might have turned toward it and its message.)

Islam is even closer in spirit to Judaism than is classical Christianity. It teaches an uncompromising monotheism and rejects the presence of any images, human or animal, in its houses of worship. Its adherents practice circumcision and do not eat pork. Its religious authorities are not priests who perform sacred rituals, but scholars of sacred law, like rabbis. Muhammad was heavily influenced by Jews whom he had known in Mecca, his birthplace in Arabia. In his early teachings he had told his followers to turn toward Jerusalem when they prayed, in the manner of the Jews. He wished them to observe the seventh day as the Sabbath and the Day of Atonement as an annual day of fasting and repentance. He changed these practices, however, when the Jews whom he approached refused to acknowledge him as the final prophet, the successor to the prophets of Israel and Jesus, who had come to prepare the way for him. The Jews of Arabia and elsewhere, except for those who embraced Islam, did not regard Muhammad as a prophet; that is, a prophet sent to *them*, because of the words of Moses in Deuteronomy 18:15: "A prophet from your midst, from your brothers, like me, will the Lord your God raise up for you." God might raise up prophets among the various nations of the world, they said, but this verse proves that the final prophet whom God will send to the Jews at the end of days will be, like Moses himself, part of the household of Israel.

From the standpoint of Judaism, it is a great sin for a Jew to become an adherent of another religion, even a monotheistic faith like Christianity or Islam. When a Jew does so, he abrogates the covenant that links him to his God and his people, the obligation that he and his descendants have to preserve the heritage initiated by Abraham. Judaism, however, looks upon Christianity and Islam as religions valid for the other nations of the world. Maimonides in the twelfth century wrote:

The teachings of the Nazarene and the Ishmaelite (Muhammad) serve the sacred purpose of preparing the way for the Messiah, who is sent to make the whole world perfect in the worship of God with one spirit; they have spread the words of the Scripture and the law of truth over the wide world, and regardless of the errors to which they may adhere, they will turn toward the full truth at the arrival of the Messianic time. (*Mishneh Torah*, Laws of Kings, 11:4)

Regarding Christianity, Jacob Emden, a rabbinic scholar in Germany during the mid-eighteenth century, wrote the following:

Christianity has been given as part of the Jewish religion by the apostles to the nations of the world; its founder made the moral laws even stricter than those contained in the religion of Moses. There are, accordingly, many Christians of high qualities and excellent morals who keep from hatred and do no harm, even to their enemies. Would that Christians would all live in conformity with their precepts! They are not enjoined, like Israel, to observe the laws of Moses, nor do they sin (as a Jew would sin) if they associate other persons with God in the worship of God as a Trinity. They will receive reward from God for having propagated a belief in Him among nations that never before heard his name.

CHAPTER FIVE

The Rabbinic Writings

The Siddur

The Siddur, the order of prayers for weekdays, Sabbaths, and holy days, began its development in the synagogues of Judea while the Temple still stood. The leaders of the rabbinic academy in Palestine and, later, the heads of the academies in Babylonia promulgated the texts of the worship services in very much the same form retained today among Orthodox Jews. Even among the non-Orthodox, the basic rubrics and much of the language continue to be the work of the early rabbis. There are minor variations distinguishing Ashkenazic liturgical traditions from Sephardic ones, as well as unique local customs throughout the world, but for the most part the text of the Orthodox Siddur is nearly identical everywhere, with the exception of some poetic insertions on the holy days. (The Judaism of Jews everywhere in the world is guided by the teachings and enactments contained in the rabbinic writings. The only exception was the Judaism of Ethiopia, which was cut off for centuries from contact with other Jews. The black Jews there possessed a Bible written not in Hebrew but in Ethiopic, so their practices were based on their interpretations of this source alone. Modern Jews did not meet with their Ethiopian colleagues until the 1860s.)

The *shaharit*, or morning service, begins with readings that are ordinarily recited privately rather than as a congregation. These include a number of blessings of thanksgiving to God, as well as the following lesson from the Mishna and Talmud:

> These are things upon which the Torah sets no fixed limit: the corners of the field (which are to be left to the poor to harvest), the offering of the first fruits, the offerings brought to the Temple on the three festivals, deeds of lovingkindness, and the study of the Torah. These are the things the interest on which a man enjoys in this world, while the principal remains for him in the world-to-come: honoring father and mother, deeds of lovingkindness, attendance at the house of study morning and evening, hospitality to wayfarers, visiting the sick, dowering the bride, accompanying the dead to the grave, devotion in prayer, making peace between man and man, and the study of the Torah which is equal to them all.

Other passages recited privately include the description of the daily sacrifices in the book of Leviticus, several psalms, and Exodus 15—the song of Moses and the Israelites after the crossing of the Red Sea.

The public service recited by the *hazzan*, or prayer leader, begins with the doxology called the *kaddish* ("sanctification"):

> Magnified and sanctified be his great name in the world which He created according to his will. May his kingdom come in your lifetime and in your days, in the life of all the house of Israel, speedily and soon, and say Amen. May his great name be blessed forever and ever and ever.

The leader then proclaims the call to worship: "Bless the Lord who is to be blessed," and the congregants respond, "Blessed is the Lord who is to be blessed forever and ever." God is then praised as the creator of light and as the loving

Father of Israel. This leads into the reading of the *shema*, the declaration of God's unity, from Deuteronomy 6:4–9:

> Hear (*shema*), Israel, the Lord is our God, the Lord is One. You shall love the Lord your God with all your heart, with all your soul, with all your might. These words which I command you this day shall be upon your heart; you shall teach them diligently to your children and talk of them when you sit in your house and when you walk by the way, when you lie down and when you rise up. You shall bind them as a sign upon your hand and they shall be frontlets between your eyes. You shall write them upon the door posts of your house and upon your gates.

The recitation of this passage is called by the rabbis "the acceptance of the yoke of the Kingdom of Heaven." The second paragraph of the *shema* is Deuteronomy 11:13–21, speaking of the rewards for those who keep God's commandments and the punishments exacted from those who do not. This the rabbis call "the acceptance of the yoke of the commandments." The third paragraph, Numbers 15:37–41, mandates the wearing of knotted fringes (*sisit*) on the corners of men's garments, to serve as reminders of the commandments. After these readings God is praised as the Redeemer of Israel, at the crossing of the Red Sea and in every generation thereafter.

The second division of the public service consists of nineteen short paragraphs (three of praise, thirteen of petition, and three additional of praise). In Orthodox practice these are recited first in silence by the congregants while they stand and then aloud by the prayer leader. In the first set of praises the first paragraph praises God as the Shield of Abraham and the other patriarchs; the second acclaims God as the one who supports the falling, heals the sick, releases the prisoners, and raises the dead; and the third celebrates his holiness. During the leader's repetition of this third paragraph of praise, the chant of the angels from Isaiah 6:3

is inserted: "Holy, holy, holy is the Lord of Hosts; the whole earth is full of his glory."

The thirteen petitions are as follows: for knowledge; for the opportunity of repentance; for forgiveness; for redemption; for the healing of the sick; for the fertility of the land; for an end to the exile; for the restoration of true judges; for the destruction of God's enemies; for the reward of the righteous; for the rebuilding of Jerusalem; for the restoration of the line of David; for the acceptance of prayer. (On the Sabbath these prayers of petition are omitted, as the Sabbath is a day of holy joy, when neither sadness nor petition are proper. They are replaced by a paragraph celebrating God as the one who hallows the Sabbath.)

The three concluding paragraphs of praise acclaim God as the one who will restore his presence to Zion, the one to whom thanks are due, and as the giver of peace.

Some prayers for forgiveness follow, concluding with the kaddish. This is followed on Monday and Thursday mornings by a reading of about ten verses from the Torah. (On the Sabbath the reading is much longer—about six chapters— and is followed by a chapter from the Prophets.) After another recitation of the kaddish, a prayer from the third century that later usage placed at the conclusion of all synagogue services is chanted:

It is our duty to praise the Lord of all, to ascribe greatness to the Author of Creation, for He did not make us like the peoples of the lands nor place us among the families of the earth. He did not set our portion among theirs nor our lot like unto their multitude. For it is we who bow and prostrate ourselves and give thanks before the King of the kings of kings, the Holy One, blessed be He. It is He who stretches out the heavens and establishes the earth. The seat of his splendor is in the heavens above and the abode of his strength is in the loftiest heights. He is our God; there is no other. Truly He is our King; there is none beside Him. As it is written in his Torah, "You shall know this day and take it to heart that the Lord He is God; in the heavens above and upon the earth beneath there is no other." We therefore wait for You, Lord our God, to see how, speedily through your glorious might, You will sweep away abominations from the earth and the idols will be utterly destroyed, how You will perfect the world by making it the Kingdom of the Almighty when all humanity will call upon your name and all the wicked of the earth will be turned to You. All the inhabitants of the earth will recognize and know that to You every knee must bend and every tongue must swear. Before You, Lord our God, they will bow and worship and give honor to your glorious name. All of them will accept the yoke of your kingdom and You will rule over them speedily and forever, for the kingdom is yours and forevermore You will reign in glory. As it is written in your Torah, "The Lord will reign forever and ever." And it is said, "The Lord will become King over all the earth; on that day the Lord will be One and his name One."

Then comes a final kaddish. Since the Middle Ages it has been customary that it is the mourners present in the congregation, rather than the prayer leader, who recite this kaddish, demonstrating thereby that, in spite of the affliction they have suffered, they still lovingly affirm the sovereignty of God. The congregation then reads the psalm for the day of the week that the Levites chanted in the Temple of Jerusalem.

The Mishna

The codification of the oral Torah was accomplished by Rabbi Judah the Prince early in the third century A.D. This is the *Mishna* ("repetition"), the basic text that has served as the source of all subsequent development of legal tradition in rabbinic Judaism. The Mishna is divided into six orders, each of which contains between seven and twelve tractates, or treatises, that summarize the laws defined by the rabbis according to specific topics. The first order is *Zeraim* ("seeds"), which deals primarily with the procedures of tithing agricultural products while the Temple was still in existence. (The first tractate of this order, however, titled *Berakot,* "benedictions," is of great importance to later Judaism since it centers about the prayer services of the synagogue.)

The second order of the Mishna is *Moed* ("festivals"), dealing with the legislation of the rabbis for the Sabbath and holy days. The third order, *Nashim* ("women"), catalogues the laws of marriage, divorce, vows, and betrothal. In the fourth order, *Nezikin* ("damages"), the rules of civil and criminal procedure are summarized, as well as laws governing the relationships of Jews to pagans and idolatrous religions. At the end of this order a very different type of tractate is appended. This is *Abot* ("fathers"), containing some of the ethical instruction and wisdom of the early rabbis. The tractate Abot is studied by children in Jewish schools from a very early age; it is also read in synagogues on the Sabbath afternoons between Passover and Pentecost.

The Mishna's fifth order is *Kodashim* ("holy things"), concentrating on the rules governing the sacrifices in the Temple. Even though the Temple had been destroyed 150 years before the promulgation of the Mishna, the rabbis were convinced that someday it would be rebuilt and that the traditions about the sacrifices should be preserved and taught. One tractate in this order, *Hullin* ("animals killed for food"), deals not with Temple matters but with the proper procedures for slaughtering animals to be eaten by Jews. The sixth order of the Mishna, *Tohorot* ("purifications"), is concerned almost exclusively with the ritual purifications that may be necessary before one is allowed to enter the precincts of the Temple. One tractate in this final order, *Nidda* ("menstruant"), is important for contemporary Orthodox Jews because it contains the laws of the rabbis that must be observed by menstruating women (based upon Leviticus 15).

The following is a sample of the style of the Mishna:

If a deaf-mute man married a woman who possessed sound senses, or if a man of sound senses married a deaf-mute woman, if he wishes he may divorce her and if he wishes he may continue the marriage. If he married her by sign language so may he divorce her by sign language. If a man of sound senses married a woman of sound senses who later became a deaf-mute, if he wishes he may divorce her and if he wishes he may continue the marriage. If she became insane he may not divorce her. If he became either a deaf-mute or insane he may never divorce her. Rabbi Johanan son of Nuri said: Why should it be that if the woman became a deaf-mute she may be divorced, but if the man became a deaf-mute he cannot divorce her? They [the other sages] answered: A man who divorces is not like a woman who is divorced, for a woman is divorced either with her consent or without it, while a husband can divorce his wife only by means of his own consent. (Yebamot 14:1)

The text assumes, of course, that a deaf-mute does not have full mental capacity. Many of the ancients, including Jews, classed deaf-mutes, together with the insane or retarded and minors, as persons incapable of making rational decisions.

Here are some of the sayings of the rabbis transmitted in the tractate Abot, at the end of the fourth order of the Mishna:

Antigonos of Soko used to say: Do not be like servants who serve their master for the sake of reward, but be like servants who serve their master without regard to the reward; and let the fear of Heaven be upon you. . . . Hillel said: Be of the disciples of Aaron, loving peace and pursuing peace, loving human creatures and bringing them near to the Torah. He used to say: A name made great is a name destroyed; he that does not increase decreases; he who does not learn is worthy of death; he who makes worldly use of the crown [of learning] shall perish. If I am not for myself who will be for me; if I am for myself alone what am I; if not now, when. . . . Simeon son of Gamaliel used to say: All my days I have grown up among the sages and I have found nothing better for a person than silence; it is not discoursing [about the Torah] that is the chief thing, but doing it; he who multiplies words multiplies sin. . . . Rabbi Johanan son of Zakkai used to say: If you have learned much Torah do not claim merit for yourself, for it was for this that you were created. . . . Rabbi Tarfon said: The day is short and the task is great; the workers are idle and the wage abundant, but the Master of the house is urgent. He used to say: It is not up to you to finish the task, but neither are you free to desist from it. . . . Rabbi Akiba used to say: Beloved is man, for he was created in the image of God; still greater was the love that made known to him that he was created in the image of God, as it is written, "In the image of God He made man." Beloved are Israel, for they were called children of God; still greater was the love that made known to them that they were called children of God, as it is written, "You are the children of the Lord your God. . . . Rabbi Simeon said: There are three crowns—the crown of Torah, the crown of priesthood, the crown of kingship; but the crown of a good name exceeds them all."

The Talmud

The Babylonian Talmud is the great compendium of Jewish law and lore. It is the major object of study in traditional rabbinical academies, and other Jews are encouraged to study it as well. It is organized into orders and tractates in the same way as the Mishna. On a page of the Talmud each paragraph of Mishna is followed by the discussions of the rabbis, both Babylonian and Palestinian, that were inspired by that paragraph. Some of these discussions ramble far and wide; others are succinct and to the point. The discussions of the rabbis are called *gemara* ("tradition"). Mishna and Gemara together constitute the Talmud. Two types of material appear in these discussions: *halaka* ("the way to go"), meaning the law decided upon by the rabbis and the analytic reasoning by which they developed the law; and *aggada* ("narration"), the nonlegal materials, including historical reminiscences, ethical insights, legends, theological speculations and even an occasional joke.

The Mishna in its presentation of the laws governing fasting on the Day of Atonement states:

> If a pregnant woman smelt food (and was overwhelmed by a compelling desire to eat) she must be given to eat until she feels restored.

As an example of a halakic discussion, the *gemara* attached to this follows:

> Our rabbis taught: If a pregnant woman smelt the flesh of consecrated food (reserved for the priests) or of pork (forbidden to Jews except when life is in danger), we put a reed into the juice and place it on her mouth. If she then feels that her craving has been satisfied, it is well. If not, we feed her with the juice itself. If she then feels that her craving is satisfied, it is well. If not, we feed her the fat meat itself, for there is no law that cannot be transgressed when it is a matter of saving life except for the prohibitions of idolatry, adultery (with a married or betrothed woman), and murder.
>
> How do we know this about idolatry? It was taught: Rabbi Eliezer said: Since it is said "you shall love the Lord with all your soul" [Deuteronomy 6:5], why does the verse add "with all your might?" And since it says "with all your might," why does it add "with all your soul"? This is to teach that if there is a person who cherishes his life more than his money, for him it is said "with all your soul"; but if there is a person whose money is dearer to him than his life, for him it is said

"with all your might" (that is, one must be willing to give
up both his life and his fortune rather than perform
idolatry).

How do we know that one must be willing to give up
life rather than commit adultery or murder? Because it
was taught: Rabbi Judah the Prince said: "This case is
like that of a man attacking and murdering his neighbor"
[Deuteronomy 22:26, referring to the rape of a betrothed
maiden]. What is the case that we infer for the rape of a
betrothed maiden from a murderer? Rather, the two
situations throw light on each other. As in the case of a
betrothed maiden it is lawful to save her at the expense
of the rapist's life, so also is the case of a murderer. And
as in the case of an order to commit murder a man must
be willing to accept death himself rather than commit
murder, so also in the case of a command to rape a
betrothed maiden one should rather be killed than do
this thing. But how do we know that this principle applies
in the case of a murder? This is reasonable. There was a
man who came before Raba and said to him: The chief-
tain of my village told me: Kill so-and-so, and if you will
not, I shall kill you. Raba answered: Let him kill you,
but do not kill (an innocent person). What makes you see
that your blood is redder than his? Perhaps the blood of
that man is redder than yours. (Yoma 82a–b)

It is not surprising to find discussions in the Talmud on
whether or not non-Jews will have a share in the world-to-
come. An example of an *aggada* ("nonlegal" discussion) on
this subject is the following:

Rabbi Eliezer had said that "none of the nations have a
share in the world-to-come," but Rabbi Joshua insisted
that "there are righteous among the nations who have a
share in the world-to-come." The Talmud (Sanhedrin
105a) preserves his reasoning. Since the Mishna lists only
Balaam as a non-Jew who will not enter the world-to-

come, we infer that "others will enter." On whose authority is this Mishna? On Rabbi Joshua's. For it has been taught: Rabbi Eliezer said, "The wicked shall depart into hell, all the nations that forget God" (Psalm 9:17). "The wicked shall depart into hell"—this refers to the sinners of Israel; "all the nations that forget God" —this refers to the non-Jews. This is Rabbi Eliezer's view. But Rabbi Joshua said to him: Does the text read "*and* all the nations"? No, it does not. What is written is "all the nations that forget God," which is to be interpreted as follows: "The wicked shall depart into hell," and who are they?—"all the people that forget God."

Rabbi Joshua thus maintained that it is only the wicked, Jewish or not, who need fear punishment in the next world. The righteous, both Jewish and non-Jewish, will be rewarded with eternal life. This being the case, one must ask how the Talmud defined righteousness for non-Jews, since they did not worship the God of Israel. The teaching is this:

Our rabbis taught: Seven precepts were the sons of Noah commanded: to establish courts of justice; to refrain from blasphemy, idolatry, adultery, murder, robbery, and eating flesh cut from a living animal. (Sanhedrin 56a)

For the rabbis these commandments constituted the basic requirements of a civilized society. The non-Jew who lived up to them was as worthy in God's sight as a Jew who lived by all the laws of the Torah (traditionally 613 in number). It was much easier, according to the thinking of the rabbis, to be righteous as a non-Jew than as a Jew, and the reward at the end of days was the same for both. We see from the Noachide commandments that the rabbis regarded kindness to animals as a universal human obligation. Talmud Shabbat 128b defines it for Jews as a commandment of the Torah so important that it can even set aside, if necessary, decrees of the rabbis.

Talmudic *aggada* also discusses the "evil impulse" with which all humans are endowed, together with their impulse toward good.

> The Holy One, blessed be He, spoke to Israel: My children, I created the Evil Impulse, but I created the Torah as its antidote; if you occupy yourselves with the Torah you will not be delivered into its hand, for it is said, "If you do well, shall you not be exalted?" (Genesis 4:7). But if you do not occupy yourselves with the Torah, you shall be delivered into its hand, for it is written, "Sin couches at the door." It is very concerned to make you sin, for it is said, "Unto you shall be its desire," but if you will it, you can rule over it, for it is said, "You shall rule over it." (Kiddushin 30b)

Though the rabbis called the impulse evil, they nevertheless acknowledged that its existence is necessary for human society.

> People once prayed, and the Tempter to Sin [the evil impulse] was delivered into their hands. They imprisoned it for three days; after that they sought for a newly laid egg to feed to an invalid throughout the whole land of Israel and could not find one. Then they said, What shall we do? Should we pray that its power be but partially destroyed? Heaven will not grant it. So they blinded it with rouge and, as a result, the average person does not lust for incestuous relationships. (Sanhedrin 64a)

The insight conveyed by this fable is that, in a world in which the sexual impulse ceases to operate, even the chickens stop laying eggs.

The rabbis regarded the evil impulse not only as the source of sexuality but also as the author of all forms of human self-assertiveness. Though they called it evil they thought of it as only partly so. In fact, it could even be called good:

It was said in the name of Rab Samuel son of Nahman: "Behold it was very good" (Genesis 1:31, God's evaluation of the created world). This refers to the good impulse, but it also refers to the evil impulse. But is the evil impulse very good? How can one say such a thing? However, were it not for the evil impulse no man would build a house or marry a wife; there would be no births or business activity. As Solomon says, "All labor and skillful work comes from a man's rivalry with his neighbor." (Ecclesiastes 4:4) (Midrash Genesis Rabba 9:9)

The rabbis taught that the evil impulse, the drive toward self-assertion, is subject to restraint by means of the Torah. The Talmud calls upon those who revere God to study and to act in accordance with his revelation as contained in the written and the oral Torah. Then, they believed, the world would truly become "very good."

The sages of the Talmud called upon humanity to imitate the acts of God Himself:

What is the meaning of the verse, "You shall walk after the Lord your God" (Deuteronomy 13:5)? Can a human being walk in the wake of the Divine Presence, for has it not been said, "The Lord your God is a devouring fire" (Deuteronomy 4:24)? But what is meant is to walk after the attributes of the Holy One, blessed be He. Just as He clothes the naked, as it is written, "The Lord God made coats of skin for Adam and Eve" (Genesis 3:21), so do you also clothe the naked. The Holy One, blessed be He, visited the sick, as it is written, "The Lord appeared unto him (Abraham) by the oaks of Mamre" (Genesis 18:1); so should you also visit the sick. The Holy One, blessed be He, comforted mourners, as it is written, "It came to pass after the death of Abraham that God blessed Isaac his son" (Genesis 25:11); so should you also comfort mourners. Just as the Holy One, blessed be He, buried the dead, as it is written, "He buried him (Moses) in the valley" (Deuteronomy 34:6), so should you also bury the dead. (Sota 14a)

Midrash

Besides the two Talmuds, Babylonian and Palestinian, the teachings of the early rabbis are contained in collections known as *midrash* ("exposition"). The literature of midrash was put together over many centuries and is in the form of comments and interpretations on biblical verses. The oldest midrashic texts concentrate upon the legal materials in Exodus, Leviticus, Numbers, and Deuteronomy. (In several instances, the midrashic sources show how the *halaka* that appears in the Talmud was developed from the Bible.) The halakic midrash on Leviticus 19:18 is as follows:

> "You shall not take revenge"—What form can vengeance take? If one man said to another, Lend me your scythe and he did not lend it to him, the next day the second man might say, Lend me your spade, and the first will answer, I will not lend it to you because you refused to lend me your scythe. For this reason it is said, "You shall not take revenge."
>
> "You shall not bear a grudge"—What form can bearing a grudge take? One said to the other, Lend me your spade, and he did not lend it to him. The next day the other said, Lend me your scythe, and the first answers, Here it is, because I am not like you, who would not lend me your spade. For this reason is it said, "You shall not bear a grudge."
>
> "You shall not take revenge or bear a grudge against the children of your people"—You take revenge by bearing a grudge against others. "You shall love your neighbor as yourself"—Rabbi Akiba said that this is the greatest principle in the Torah. Ben Azzai said that an even greater principle is expressed in the words "This is the book of the generations of man." (since it emphasizes the common kinship of all humanity.) (Sifra 89a-b)

Another midrash, Genesis Rabba 24:8, includes a fuller comment by Rabbi Akiba on the command "Love your neighbor as yourself":

> Let no one say, since I am despised, let my neighbor be despised with me; since I am cursed, let my neighbor be cursed with me. Rabbi Tanhuma added, One who acts like this should know whom he actually despises, since "in the image of God did He make him."

The concern of the rabbinic tradition that the love of neighbor be placed at the very center of religious consciousness is brought out clearly by the well-known story of Hillel in the Talmud:

> Once a heathen came before Shammai and said to him, "Make me a proselyte to Judaism on condition that you teach me the whole Torah while I stand on one foot." He repulsed him with the builder's tool that he was holding in his hand. When he came before Hillel, he said to him, "What is hateful to you, do not do to your neighbor: that is the whole Torah; the rest is commentary upon it; now go and learn." (Shabbat 31a)

Most of the midrashic collections are not concerned with *halaka,* but rather with *aggada.* They preserve legends and, on occasion, history about biblical figures and a good many of the Palestinian rabbis. Plays on words, hard to reproduce in translation, are quite common. Many of the texts are homilies or sermons, or excerpts from sermons, that demonstrate the ingenuity of the preachers and their ability to weave together verses from various biblical books for the purpose of teaching a lesson, or giving inspiration or comfort. An example of aggadic midrash is provided by Exodus Rabba 1:3:

> "These are the names of the children of Israel who came to Egypt with Jacob; each one came with his household."

Israel is equated with the host of heaven. Just as here the word "names" is used, so with regard to the stars is the word "names" used, as it is said, "He counts the number of the stars; he calls them all by names" (Psalm 147:4). So did the Holy One, blessed be He, when Israel went down to Egypt, count their number, seeing how many they were and, since they are compared to the stars, he called them all by name. Thus is it written, "These are the names of the children of Israel."

Responsa

The completion and dissemination of the Babylonian Talmud into Jewish communities throughout the world inspired scholars to write commentaries upon the text, with the aim of resolving ambiguities, correcting erroneous readings, and applying the tactics of talmudic discussion to new situations. Several of these commentaries are routinely printed in the standard editions of the Talmud.

The scholars who authored these commentaries also conducted a voluminous correspondence with rabbis in various parts of the Jewish world. These letters, as well as those by other authorities, are called "questions and answers," or *responsa,* and have been circulated, first in manuscript and subsequently in printed form, among rabbis far and wide. The responsa deal with the same subjects that are discussed in the commentaries, although, of course, a great many of them are concerned with the application of talmudic law to new conditions and circumstances in Jewish communities far removed from ancient Palestine and Babylonia. Questions and answers were sent between Palestine and Babylonia even before the redaction of the two Talmuds. Thereafter, the heads of the Babylonian academies authored thousands of responsa, many of which have come down to later times. Because there is no system of hierarchical government in Judaism since the Palestinian and Babylonian academies ceased, no rabbi by virtue of his office can order another rabbi to adopt a particular interpretation of law. For this reason, the influence exerted by responsa came to be quite important in standardizing many aspects of Jewish practice. The rabbis to whom questions were addressed were men universally respected for their acuity of intellect and their devotion to faith and tradition. Those who addressed questions to them accepted their responses not because the respondents held any particular office, but because they were people of unimpeachable wisdom and integrity whose judgment could be relied upon. This is still the practice in Orthodox Judaism. Rabbis send their questions to senior colleagues whom they revere and respect, and their written replies become part of the body of tradition that can be transmitted to future generations. In Conservative Judaism questions are usually directed to the Law Committee of the Rabbinical Assembly, and rabbis are free to be guided by either the majority or minority report of that committee. In Reform Judaism responsa are written also, although *halaka* is not considered binding by most Reform rabbis and the recommendations of Reform respondents are advisory only.

An interesting and representative responsum by Rabbenu Hananel of Kairwan (North Africa, eleventh century) reads as follows:

> You have asked whether the talmudic saying that it is better to let the children of Israel transgress laws unconsciously that they would transgress consciously if they were to be fully instructed about them, is not contradictory to many passages of Scripture, such as "You shall certainly rebuke your neighbor" (Leviticus 19:17), "If you warn the wicked of his way" (Ezekiel 33:9), "To them that rebuke him shall be delight" (Proverbs 24:5). This is my answer: It is true that the children of Israel are commanded to rebuke one another and so it is written by the prophets and the sages, referring to either one person or a community that is guilty of a transgression. If a violation of the words of the Torah is conscious, the transgressor must be warned and, if necessary, he may be

punished, while, on the other hand, every effort must be made to win him back to righteousness. If, however, all this is without avail, then as Ezekiel wrote, "You have delivered your soul." In case the transgression is unconscious and there is reason to suppose that the children of Israel would obey if they were instructed, they must be warned and enlightened concerning the teachings of the Torah and the way of righteousness. It is otherwise, however, when what is forbidden is regarded as permitted, and when a prohibition is taken with little seriousness because it is assumed that there is no violation of the Torah. Thus, on the eve of the Day of Atonement people sit at a meal in broad daylight, and the meal lasts until evening draws near. Those who eat intend to finish the meal in due time [before the fast must begin] and wish to fix the proper moment arbitrarily. They say "It is still time" while darkness is approaching and, though we should warn them, they would not listen. In such cases it is better for us to remain silent, and not allow them to become guilty of conscious sin. This case is different from one in which we see someone transgress a law consciously, for then we are duty-bound to lift our voices against him on the chance that he will listen to us.

Codes

After the promulgation of the Talmud, the rabbis—the interpreters of the Jewish legal tradition—utilized it as the source of law with which to govern their respective communities. It was not always easy, though, to find clear legal decisions in the Talmud because it is a vast work, replete with discussion and argumentation about the law, as well as much archaic and nonlegal material. This is one reason why many rabbis relied on responsa for answers to complex questions. There were many rabbis who yearned for a simple code of law that they could consult, but others were vehement in their opposition. They said that the promulgation of a code of Jewish law would demean the position and function of a rabbi; he would become little more than a clerk, looking up what he needed to know in an index. They feared that the presence of a code would wean rabbis away from their immersion in the Talmud and the intellectual prowess that that requires.

Moses Maimonides in the twelfth century put together the *Mishneh Torah* ("repetition of the Torah"), a great compendium of Jewish law. In this work he advocates that the righteous person adopt the "golden mean" in both emotions and acts. For instance, we should be neither easily angered nor unfeeling. We should not desire luxuries but rather acquire things that we genuinely need. We should give charity to others, but not impoverish ourselves in doing so. We should avoid both irrational gaiety and deep depression, cultivating instead an attitude of serenity. He also enumerated the eight ways in which charity to the poor might be bestowed:

There are eight degrees or steps in the duty of charity. The first and lowest degree is to give, but with reluctance or regret. This is the gift of the hand, but not of the heart. The second is to give cheerfully, but not proportionately to the distress of the sufferer. The third is to give cheerfully and proportionately, but not until solicited. The fourth is to give cheerfully, proportionately and even unsolicited, but to put it in the poor man's hand and thus excite in him the painful feeling of shame.

The fifth is to give charity in such a way that the distressed may receive the bounty and know their benefactor, without their being known to him. Such was the conduct of some of our ancestors who would tie up money in the corners of their cloaks so that the poor might take it unperceived. The sixth, which rises still higher, is to know the objects of our bounty, but remain unknown to them. Such was the conduct of those of our ancestors who used to bring their charitable gifts into poor people's homes, taking care that their own identities

would remain unknown. The seventh is still more meritorious; to bestow charity in such a way that the benefactor
will not know who receives his gifts, nor will the recipient
know the name of his benefactor. This was done by our
ancestors when the Temple still stood. In that holy building there was a place called the Chamber of the Silent,
where the generous would deposit in secret whatever
they wished and the poor would withdraw support with
equal secrecy.

The last, the eighth degree, the most meritorious of
all, is to anticipate need by preventing poverty; that is,
by assisting one in need by means of a considerable gift,
or a loan of money, or by teaching him a trade, or by
putting him in the way of business, so that he might earn
an honest livelihood and not be forced to hold out his
hand for charity. To this Scripture alludes when it says:
"If your brother becomes poor and cannot maintain himself with you, you shall maintain him; whether he be a
stranger or a sojourner he shall live with you" (Deuteronomy
25:35). This is the highest step and the summit of charity's golden ladder. (*Mishneh Torah,* Laws of Gifts to the
Poor, 10:7–13).

By the sixteenth century opposition to the idea of a legal
code had died away, so one that came to be accepted as
authoritative by Jewish communities throughout the world
was promulgated. This code was the work of Joseph Karo,
who was part of the mystical Jewish community in Safed in
Palestine. It is called the *Shulhan Aruk,* meaning "the set
table," and it sets forth in concise and clear form the laws
and customs followed in the Jewish communities of its day.
Karo's code dealt with Sephardic practice but when Moses
Isserles of Poland added glosses and additions, called "the
tablecloth," to cover Ashkenazic practice, the Shulhan Aruk
became acceptable for Jews everywhere. It is the authoritative statement of Orthodox Jewish law to this day, governing practically every detail of one's life.

Karo's code, following the example of some of its predecessors, is organized in four main divisions or "pillars": *Orah Hayyim* ("The Path of Life"), describing daily prayers and the rules for Sabbath and holy days; *Yoreh Deah* ("Teacher of Knowledge"), containing the laws of permitted and forbidden things, including dietary laws, the rite of circumcision, and death and burial practices: *Eben haEzer* ("The Stone of Help"), including the rules of sexual relations, marriage, and divorce; and *Hoshen Mishpat* ("The Breastplate of Judgment"), detailing the laws of contracts and commerce.

The following regulations appear in Shulhan Aruk Orah Hayyim, Laws Concerning the Blessing after a Meal, 184–186:

One who eats at a particular place is obligated to offer the blessing [of thanks] before he removes himself from that place. If he left his place without blessing on purpose, he must return to the place and offer the blessing; if, however, he offers the blessing at the spot where he remembered [his obligation], he has fulfilled it. If he left by accident, according to Maimonides he may recite the blessing at the place where he remembers his obligation; Rabbenu Asher, however, says that even he should return to the spot where he ate and offer the blessing. To what do these rules refer? To the case where he has no bread left (having eaten it all at the meal). If, however, he has some bread on hand he may eat some at the place where he remembers his obligation and bless, provided that he is not already hungry (it being so long a time) from the original meal. . . . He who has eaten and does not remember if he blessed or not is obligated to bless out of doubt, since the obligation to bless after a meal is from the Torah. . . . The blessing after the meal may be recited in any language. . . . Women are obligated to recite the blessing, though there is a doubt as to whether their obligation derives from the Torah so that their recital of the blessing can fulfill the obligation of men who participate in the meal, or whether they are obligated only according to the teaching of the rabbis and hence qualified to fulfill the obligation only of those whose own obligation derives from the rabbis.

In these days, when there is much discussion of how a terminally ill patient should be treated, the halaka given in the Shulhan Aruk is very instructive:

A moribund person is like one alive in all respects. . . . We do not close his eyes until the soul has departed. Whoever closes his eyes before it is certain that the soul has departed is like one who sheds blood. . . . It is forbidden to actively hasten the death of one who is dying, as in the case of someone who has been moribund for a long time with the soul being unable to separate [from the body]. It is forbidden to remove the mattress or pillow under him, because some say that the feathers of certain birds (that might escape from the bedclothes) can cause this to happen. It is also forbidden to move him from his place or place the keys of the synagogue under his head [a folk belief held that this could hasten death] so that the soul might separate. But if there is something that prevents the departure of the soul, like the sound of knocking in the vicinity of the house, for example the chopping of wood, or if there is salt on his tongue, and it is one of these factors that prevents the departure of the soul, it is permitted to take it away. For this act consists of nothing more than the removal of an obstacle." (Yoreh Deah, Laws Concerning Visiting the Sick, Healing, and the Dying, 339)

Thus, in the case of terminally ill person, it is forbidden to actively hasten his death. If, however, there is an extraneous cause that seemingly retards death from taking place, that cause may be removed. The question that contemporary halakists must face is whether the removal of an artificial respirator or of intravenous feeding or medication from a terminally ill patient constitutes actively hastening his death or is merely the removal of an extraneous obstacle to death.

Since the promulgation of the Shulhan Aruk there has been no new Jewish code of law. What have been published from time to time, are digests of the Shulhan Aruk or commentaries upon it. The development of halaka during the past 400 years has been accomplished not through new codes but through the publication of responsa literature. This never ceases, since questions are forever being asked and, in most cases, answers, whether tentative or definitive, are offered by the scholars of halaka. For some time there has been talk of a "code of law," or an authoritative "guide," that might be used by Reform Jews or by the Conservatives or Reconstructionists, but nothing of this type has ever been published by an official rabbinic body.

CHAPTER SIX

Philosophy and Mysticism

The Bible and the rabbinic writings do not contain any systematic analysis of the nature of God, the world, or the human race. It was only when the Jews came in contact with groups whose scholars speculated about these matters that Jewish thinkers were stimulated to compare their own biblical and rabbinic tradition with the ideas that were current in the societies in which they lived. The first Jewish philosopher was Philo of Alexandria, a great hellenistic city where the teachings of Plato were studied and revered. Philo's writings, however, were not known to Jews who did not speak Greek, and it is only in modern times that his works have been reclaimed as part of the Jewish heritage.

The great efflorescence of Jewish philosophical writing began in the tenth century among Jews who resided in the Islamic world. Muslim scholars had translated the works of the Greek philosophers into Arabic, and Jews immersed themselves in these texts—some as Neo-Platonists and some as Aristotelians—and wrote extensively about the general congruence between the insights of the philosophers and the teachings of the Bible and the rabbis. The selections from the philosophers presented in this chapter do not pretend to cover the development of Jewish philosophy in a systematic fashion. The thinkers who are discussed are among the best known, but there were a great many others who made important contributions. A number of them influenced the Christian philosophic tradition, as well as the Islamic. For the most part, the Jewish philosophers were strictly orthodox in their attitude toward religious belief and practice; their works are acceptable for study in the academies of all branches of Judaism. In the seventeenth century, however, Baruch Spinoza, from the Sephardic community in Amsterdam, a brilliant student of the works of the Jewish thinkers who had preceded him, was excommunicated for advocating heretical ideas. He was a pantheist and cast doubt on the Mosaic authorship of the Torah in his writings. Thus, Orthodox religious authority was able to place limits on how far philosophic speculation could go. Spinoza achieved posthumous fame not as a "Jewish" philosopher, but as one who helped initiate the modern era of philosophic thought.

At the same time that rationalistic philosophic speculation was flourishing among the Jews of Spain and, later, within the Sephardic dispersion, so, too, were many mystical texts being written. The mystical tradition, which goes back to Babylonian Jewry and perhaps even to ancient Israel, seeks to expound the "secret" meanings of the Torah. Jewish mysticism does not seek to reject or deny the teachings of the rationalist philosophers; rather it seeks to supplement them with an exposition of the deeper mysteries of the Torah for those who are prepared to receive them. The Torah, it has been taught, has many faces. An understanding of the simple meaning of the Torah is necessary, as well as the homiletic and allegorical. The rationalist philosophers are helpful in illuminating these forms of understanding. But, according to the Jewish mystical philosophers, after one had mastered this level of understanding he can go on to the "secret" teachings. One who reached this level was deemed to have entered the *pardes* ("paradise"), an acronym formed from the Hebrew terms for the four major forms of expounding the Torah.

During the nineteenth and early twentieth centuries a number of Jewish philosophers lived, studied, and wrote in

Germany. Most of them had no interest in the mystical tradition; they were attached, rather, to German idealism, particularly the teachings of Immanuel Kant and his successors. Their work has been important in developing a philosophic foundation for contemporary, non-Orthodox forms of Judaism.

Early Philosophers

Philo

Philo, who lived during the first century, was an Alexandrian Jew who sought to allegorize the Bible in terms of Plato's philosophy. He wrote voluminously in Greek. He reconciled Plato's concept of the eternal Ideas with biblical theology by introducing the *Logos* (Greek for "word" or "reason") as the intermediary between God, who is pure spirit and therefore all good, and the world, which is matter and hence potentially evil. God Himself is absolutely transcendent, relating to humanity through his Kingly and Creative potencies. For Philo, Abraham, Isaac, and Jacob were not only real people, they were also "living laws." Abraham is the symbol of the attainment of perfection through revelation; Isaac is the symbol of inherited perfection (since he is the offspring of Abraham and Sarah, who is defined as "queenly virtue"); and Jacob represents the attainment of perfection through practice and hard struggle.

Here is Philo's treatment of the creation of Adam:

> "And God formed the man by taking clay from the earth and breathed into his face a breath of life, and the man became a living soul" (Genesis 2:7). There are two types of men: the one a heavenly man, the other earthly. The heavenly man, being made after the image of God, is altogether without part or lot in corruptible and terrestrial substance; but the earthly one was compacted out of the matter scattered here and there, which Moses calls

"clay." For this reason he says that the heavenly man was not molded, but was stamped with the image of God; while the earthly is a molded work of the (divine) Artificer, but not his offspring. We must account the man made out of the earth to be mind mingling with, but not yet blended with, body. But this earthlike mind is in reality also corruptible, were not God to breathe into it a power of real life; when He does so, it does not any more undergo molding, but becomes a soul, not an inefficient and imperfectly formed soul, but one endowed with mind and actually alive; for he says, "man became a living soul." (*Allegorical Interpretation of Genesis,* I, 31–32)

Saadia

Saadia lived during the first half of the tenth century in Babylonia, where he was the head of one of the great rabbinic academies with the title *gaon* ("excellency"). He was the first Jewish thinker to write a systematic philosophic treatise in the manner of those composed by Muslim philosophers. Saadia's great work was *The Book of Beliefs and Opinions,* written in Arabic and subsequently translated into Hebrew. Saadia maintained that the truths of revelation are derived through reason, the sources of truth being four in number: sense perception; self-evident truths (including basic ethical ideals); logical inference (the basis of scientific thought); and religious tradition. He derives the existence of God from the concept of the creation of the world, which, he says, could not have come into being by itself. This Creator-God is living, omnipotent, and omniscient, although any positive statements we make about God or attributes we apply to Him really imply no more than the negation of their opposites. The only thing that we can truly assert in a positive sense about God is that He *is.* Saadia divides the commandments of the Torah between the rational ones, whose underlying reasons we know, and the revealed ones, whose basis we cannot so easily discern. These revealed commandments include the consecration of certain days, the consecration of certain people as prophets or priests, the prohibition of certain foods, the prohibition of sexual relations with certain people, and the isolation required upon the occurrence of ritual defilement. Even with regard to these matters, however, it is possible to speculate about the possible reasons behind them.

Saadia says that God has foreknowledge of all things that will occur, but this knowledge does not cause them to occur.

> Someone might perhaps ask: "If it be true that God does not desire the rebellion of the rebellious, how is it possible that there should exist in his world anything that He does not approve of or find pleasure in?" The answer to this is quite simple. If it seems odd to us that one who is all-wise should permit anything to transpire in his domain that does not accord with his wishes or please him, that could apply only to man. For when a human being hates a thing, he does so usually because it harms him. Our God, however, does not hate anything on account of his own personality, because it is impossible that He be affected by any of the accidents appertaining to mortals. He considers them objectionable only on our account, because of the harm they might inflict on us. For if we transgress against Him by failing to acknowledge our indebtedness to Him, we are guilty of folly. On the other hand, if we wrong one another, we bring about the destruction of our lives and our wealth. (*Book of Beliefs and Opinions*, IV, 4)

Judah haLevi

Judah haLevi, the greatest Hebrew poet of the "golden age" in Spain, lived during the first half of the twelfth century. His philosophical work is contained in the book *Kuzari*, written in Arabic and subsequently translated into Hebrew. The book draws its inspiration from a historical occurrence: the conversion to Judaism of the royal house of the Khazar kingdom that lay between the Caspian and Black

Seas during the eighth century. In his book haLevi portrays the king of the Khazars as inquiring of a secular philosopher and representatives of Christianity and Islam, concluding that, for him at least, their interpretations of life and the world were not fully satisfying. He then consults a rabbi, since both Christianity and Islam regard Judaism as the basis for their own teachings. The king embraces Judaism and takes further instruction from the rabbi. HaLevi's *Kuzari* is, for the most part, the explication of Judaism given by the rabbi to the king. In it he dwells at length on the place of the Jewish people in the world:

> Israel among the nations is like the heart among the organs of the body. It is at one and the same time the sickest and the healthiest of them. The heart is exposed to all sorts of diseases, and is frequently visited by them, such as sadness, anxiety, wrath, envy, enmity, love, hate, and fear. Its temperament changes continually, undulating between excess and deficiency, and is influenced by inferior nourishment, by movement, exertion, sleep, or wakefulness. They all affect the heart while the limbs rest. . . . Just as the heart is pure in substance and matter, and of even temperament, in order to be accessible to the intellectual soul (that resides in the body), so also is Israel in its component parts. In the same way as the heart may be affected by disease of the other organs— lusts of the liver, stomach, and genitals caused through contact with malignant elements—so also is Israel exposed to its ills originating in its inclining toward the ways of the nations. As it is said, "They were mingled among the nations and learned their works" (Psalm 106:35). Do not consider it strange if, in the same manner, it is said, "Surely he has borne our griefs and carried our sorrows" (Isaiah 53:4). Now we are burdened by them, while the whole world enjoys rest and prosperity. The trials that meet us are meant to prove our faith, to cleanse us completely, and remove all taint from us. If we are good, the Divine Influence is with us in this

world. You know that the elements gradually evolved
into metals, plants, animals, man, and finally the pure
essence of man. This whole evolution took place for the
sake of this essence, in order that the Divine Influence
should inhabit it. That essence, in fact, came into existence for the sake of the highest essence; that is to say,
the prophets and the pious. (*Kuzari,* II, 36–44)

HaLevi taught that only Jews are capable of becoming
prophets and that prophecy can only occur in, or be concerned with, the land of Israel. In the end of days,

God has a secret and wise design concerning us [Israel],
which should be compared to the wisdom hidden in the
seed which falls to the ground where it undergoes an
external transformation into earth, water, and dirt, without leaving a trace for him who looks upon it. It is the
seed itself which transforms earth and water into its own
substance, carrying it from one degree to another, until it
refines the elements and transfers them into something like
itself, casting off husks and leaves and allowing the pure
core to appear, capable of bearing the Divine Influence.
The original seed produced the tree bearing fruit that
resembles that from which it had been produced. In the
same manner the Torah of Moses transforms each one
who honestly follows it, though it may externally repel
him. The nations merely serve to introduce and pave the
way for the expected Messiah, who is the fruition, and
they will all become his fruit. Then, if they acknowledge
him, they will become one tree. Then they will revere the
origin which they formerly despised, as it is said, "Behold
my servant prospers" [Isaiah 52:13]. (*Kuzari,* IV, 23)

Moses Maimonides

Moses Maimonides lived during the latter half of the
twelfth century. Born in Spain, he lived the greater part of
his life in Egypt. He functioned as a physician and official of

the Jewish community, and wrote numerous responsa, a commentary to the Mishna, and a masterly code of Jewish law. He also wrote several philosophical treatises, including the acclaimed *Guide to the Perplexed*. Maimonides was an Aristotelian, forging a harmony between biblical ideas and Aristotle's rationalism. He asserted, for instance, that God has no need of the animal sacrifices prescribed by the Torah. They were included among the commandments only because this was the sole mode of worship that would have been comprehensible to people in ancient times. Maimonides is regarded to this day as the greatest mind in medieval Judaism.

Maimonides maintained that God is absolutely incorporeal and that any Jew who believes literally in the biblical phrases that imply corporeality in God is a heretic. When man is said to have been created in the image of God, the meaning is that he has the ability to grasp the intellectual forms of reality by means of pure mind. The essential attributes of God, Maimonides said, are unknowable. When we say that God is holy, all knowing, all powerful, we assert nothing more than the negation of the opposites of these terms. However, we are able to know God's ethical attributes in a positive sense, since these constitute the *ways* of God in his dealings with us. Hence, in the sphere of ethics, it is possible to imitate God, and this we are commanded to do.

Like Aristotle, Maimonides defines God as the First Cause and the Prime Mover. There must be a First Cause because an infinite series is impossible in a logical sense. The universe is ordered, lawful, with all things in constant motion in the sense of movement from potentiality to actuality. Maimonides parted from Aristotle in asserting that the world was created out of nothing at a definite moment in time. While the Greek philosopher had maintained that the universe was eternal because all becoming is the putting off of one form and the taking on of another, Maimonides argued that this would not necessarily be so until the world had come into being. Aristotle had also argued that God could not have created the world because that would have implied a certain need or insufficiency in Him; to this Maimonides rejoined that while such needs are present in human beings, it is not necessary to apply these same categories to God.

The metaphysical realm, said Maimonides, operates according to the will of God. The physical realm operates in accordance with divinely ordained law. He explained the miracles recounted in the Scriptures either as preordained suspensions of natural law already arranged at Creation, or as human modes of speech that were not meant to be understood in a literal way. (A good portion of the *Guide to the Perplexed* is devoted to a minute analysis of biblical terminology and the author's explanations of the miracles in the Hebrew Scriptures in rational terms.) Even prophecy is not understood as a "miracle." The prophet, according to Maimonides, is one who is able, through his imaginative faculty, to bring himself into contact with the Active Intellect of God. The prophet's intellectual attainment, plus his imaginative faculty, enable him to have flashes of insight. Moses was the chief of the prophets, although philosophers of all nations, not just Jews, are eligible to receive this gift. (Here, of course, Maimonides differs radically from the view of Judah haLevi.) Human immortality is the result of a person's intellectual attainment, the union of the activated intellectual mind with the Active Intellect of God. Since not everyone has the intellectual capacity to become a philosopher, Maimonides allowed that lesser types might strive to attain immortality by subscribing to the correct beliefs defined by the Jewish philosophers in addition to living by the commandments.

Maimonides was among the first to systematically define the basic theology of Judaism. This he formulated as the "thirteen principles of faith." These principles, which are still accepted as authoritative by Orthodox Judaism, were presented by Maimonides in his Commentary to Mishna Sanhedrin 10:1. The text that follows is the shortened version included for private meditation in the Orthodox Siddur.

1. I believe with perfect faith that the Creator, blessed be his name, is the creator and guide of everything that has been created, and that He alone did make, does make, and will make all things.

2. I believe with perfect faith that the Creator, blessed be his name, is a Unity, and that there is no unity in any manner like his, and that He alone is our God who was, who is, and will be.

3. I believe with perfect faith that the Creator, blessed be his name, is not a body, that He is free from all bodily accidents and has no form whatsoever.

4. I believe with perfect faith that the Creator, blessed be his name, is the first and the last.

5. I believe with perfect faith that to the Creator, blessed be his name, to Him alone, is it right to pray, and that it is not right to pray to any besides Him.

6. I believe with perfect faith that all the words of the prophets are true.

7. I believe with perfect faith that the prophecy of Moses our teacher, peace be unto him, was true, and that he was the chief of the prophets, both those who came before him and those who followed him.

8. I believe with perfect faith that the entire Torah now found in our hands is what was given to Moses our teacher, peace be unto him.

9. I believe with perfect faith that this Torah will not be changed, nor will there be another Torah from the Creator, blessed be his name.

10. I believe with perfect faith that the Creator, blessed be his name, knows all the deeds of men and all their thoughts, as it is said, "He forms their hearts together, He understands all their deeds" (Psalm 33:15).

11. I believe with perfect faith that the Creator, blessed be his name, rewards those who keep his commandments and punishes those who transgress his commandments.

12. I believe with perfect faith in the coming of the Messiah and, though he tarry, in spite of all this I will await him daily, that he should come.

13. I believe with perfect faith that there will be a resurrection of the dead at a time when it shall please the Creator, blessed be his name and exalted be his remembrance forever and ever.

Mysticism

Zohar

Not all the scholars among the Jews of Spain cultivated the rationalistic philosophic approach to which Maimonides and others were devoted. There were those who embraced the Jewish mystical tradition, the study of the secret lore that could open the mysteries of the Scriptures to those who were properly instructed. No doubt there were secret teachings that went far back into antiquity, and mystical texts were known from the community in Babylonia; but it was within Spanish Jewry that mystical speculation underwent its greatest development. Only men who were learned in all the other branches of Jewish knowledge (Scripture and rabbinic texts), and who were piously observant of religious law, were eligible to go on to the study of the *kabbala*, the arcane texts. In addition, they had to be married and at least thirty years of age.

The greatest work of the kabbala, which captured the imagination of those who delved into it from its appearance and continues to do so to the present, is the *Zohar*, the book of Splendor. The Zohar purports to be the work of Rabbi Simeon son of Yohai, a sage from second-century Palestine, but modern scholars are convinced it is the work of Moses de Leon, from thirteenth-century Spain. Although de Leon is its author in its present form, the text no doubt contains some very old materials. Most of it is written in a rather stylized Aramaic in an attempt to imitate the language of the second century.

Much of the Zohar is a commentary to the books of the Torah, interpreting biblical language and events in terms of the ten emanations (*sefirot*) in which God unfolded Himself and by means of which He creates all things. The *sefirot* are the following:

1. *Crown*, the most recondite of all, the source from which all else comes; the first effulgence of light out of the primal darkness, which is the "nothingness" that is the ultimate source of God Himself.
2. *Wisdom*, the masculine element called Father or Beginning, the active potency that engenders all else.
3. *Understanding*, the feminine element called Mother, that which receives Wisdom within and gives birth to the seven remaining *sefirot* that correspond to the seven days of creation.
4. *Kindness*, the manifestation of the masculine element in the lower *sefirot*, linked to Abraham.
5. *Rigor*, the opposite of Kindness, the harsh judgment or punishment that is the major manifestation of the feminine element in the lower *sefirot*, linked to Isaac.
6. *Beauty*, the union of Kindness and Rigor that constitutes the Tree of Life, identified with the Torah and with Heaven, linked to Jacob and the sun.
7. *Victory*, the vigor that congregates on the right side, enabling God to subjugate his enemies and rescue the righteous.
8. *Majesty*, the corresponding vigor of the left side. Victory and Majesty are linked to Moses and Aaron.
9. *Foundation*, the element into which all the potencies and excellence flow; the consummation and result of all the preceding *sefirot*, linked to Joseph and the covenant of circumcision.
10. *Kingdom*, who is the Female, the Bride, the Community of Israel, the Sabbath, Earth, Jerusalem. She is linked to David and is sometimes called the Tree

of the Knowledge of Good and Evil that can become the Tree of Death. She is styled most often, however, as the Shekina, that aspect of divinity which, according to the early rabbis, dwelt in the Temple of Jerusalem and, upon its destruction, went into exile with her people. Though ideally the Shekina should be united, on the analogy of the Father and Mother above, with the Holy King (who is the union of the six *sefirot* directly above her), while the exile lasts they are able to come together only on the Sabbath. The Shekina's symbol is the moon, which, having no light of its own, must be illumined by the sun (Beauty).

Kabbala in general, including the Zohar, lavishes a great deal of attention on the letters of the Hebrew alphabet, and on various combinations and permutations thereof. The letters are regarded as the very instruments of creation. The letters of the divine name *YHWH* play a special role and are related to the *sefirot* in the following manner: the *Y* (Hebrew letter *yod*), the smallest letter in the alphabet, begins its manifestation in Crown and develops to its fullness in Wisdom. It then brings forth the *H* (Hebrew letter *hey*), which is Understanding. *Y* and *H* come together as Father and Mother, giving birth to the Son and Daughter, which are *W* (Hebrew letter *waw*) and the second *H* of YHWH. The *W*, since it serves in Hebrew as the numeral "six," refers to the six *sefirot* comprising the Holy King, while the second *H* is his Bride, the Shekina. The *H*, both upper and lower, provides the breath of life that animates all things. From the Mother the breath comes to the Bride, and through the Bride the material world is sustained. In the process of divine evolution the *sefirot* and the letters of the Name are supposed to be in balance and equilibrium. Face should gaze upon face, with God in his male aspect united with God in his female aspect; all should radiate peace and joy. It is when the union of these finely balanced elements is disrupted that suffering and wrath come into the world.

The Zohar builds much of its teaching upon the assertion

in Genesis that man was created in the image of God. It derives from this the idea that God, particularly the Holy King with his Shekina, can be understood in the image of man. In fact, it regards "Adam" as one of God's names. Since Adam is also the name for generic man, in the Zohar's conception the male united with the female, the inference is that he mirrors the Divine Form. "Adam is the form that includes all forms; Adam is the name that includes all names. In Adam are concealed all the worlds, both above and below. In Adam are all the secrets that were uttered or established before the world was created, even those that have never come to pass."

When the male is sundered from the female, woe to the world, for what occurs in the lower world is but a reflection of what takes place above. The Zohar interprets the fall of man in the Garden of Eden as revealing not only the exiled condition of humanity on earth, but that of the Supernal Adam as well, separated from his Shekina:

> Everywhere Adam is male and female, the Holy Supernal Adam ruling over all and giving sustenance and life to all. Thus from all did the mighty serpent cause the light to be withheld. When it pollutes the tabernacle, the female of that Adam dies and the male dies also, and they both return to the state in which they had been before being formed as Adam (that is, a state of imbalance and disequilibrium). Thus what is below corresponds to what is above. (Zohar II, 144b)

The Zohar has attracted so many over the centuries because if, as it teaches, God experiences the exiled state of man, then there is all the more reason to expect that one day the exile will come to an end and both God and man will be whole and complete once more. The solution that it offers for the problem of both God and man is that the Jew must observe the commandments of the Torah, the Tree of Life, with full and proper and dedicated intention (kavvana). In this way will the permanent reunion of the King with his

Shekina be hastened. In the meantime, the Jew on the Sabbath must experience the joy of union and perfection, for on this day, even in this imperfect and polluted world, the King and the Bride come together, harsh judgment is assuaged, and all things taste of the joys of Eden. The banquet on the Sabbath night is in honor of the Shekina, for this is her wedding feast, the time when she is united with her spouse. The banquet at Sabbath noon is in honor of the Holy Ancient One, the *sefirot* Crown, Wisdom, and Understanding, for in its eternal joy it encompasses and comprehends all. The banquet at the Sabbath afternoon, just before the sun sets, is in honor of the King for, although on the days of the week it is at this hour that He sits in judgment, on the Sabbath his proclivity to judgment is assuaged. When all are in union and in equilibrium, Kindness rules over all and then, as Rabbi Simeon said, "The Lord commanded the blessing, life forevermore."

The style of the Zohar is illustrated by the following passage:

If the righteous truly knew all, they would rejoice on the day assigned to them to leave this world. For is it not a high honor that the Matrona (the Shekina) comes on their account, to bring them to the King's palace, that the King may rejoice in them every day? For to the Holy One, blessed be He, there is no joy except in the souls of the righteous. Come and see: It is the souls of the righteous here below that arouse the love of the Community of Israel (the Shekina) for the Holy One, blessed be He, for they come from the side of the King, the side of the male. This arousal goes to the female and awakens her love for the male. Thus does the male stir the love and tenderness of the female, and the female is united with the male in love. In like manner the female's desire to pour forth waters below to mingle with waters above is incited only through the souls of the righteous. Happy are the righteous in this world and in the world-to-come, for on them are the upper and lower beings established. Thus is it said, "The righteous is the foundation of the world" (Proverbs 10:25). (Zohar, I, 245b)

The Zohar considers the plight of innocent children who die in this affecting passage:

Solomon said: "So I returned and considered all the oppressed who were made under the sun, and behold the tears of these who were oppressed and they had no comforter" (Ecclesiastes 4:1). He reflected and said: I consider the sad fate of these hapless oppressed who had been "made," how they shed tears before the Holy One. They complain before Him and moan, saying, When a person sins he must surely die. But, Sovereign of the world, when a child is but one day old, shall he be judged? These are the tears of the oppressed, who have no comforter. There are many different kinds among them, but they all shed tears. There is, for instance, the child born of adultery. As soon as he emerges into the world he is separated from the community of the holy people and he laments and sheds tears before the Holy One and complains: Lord of the world, if my parents have sinned, where is my guilt? I have tried to do only good works before You. But the greatest grief of all emanates from those "oppressed" who are but little sucklings that have been removed from their mothers' breasts. These can indeed cause the whole world to weep, and there are no tears like theirs, for these are tears that come from the inmost and deepest recesses of the heart, causing the whole world to wonder and say: The Holy One's judgments are ever righteous and all his paths are ways of truth. But why is it necessary for these poor little ones, who are blameless and without sin, to die? Where is now the true and righteous judgment of the Lord of the world? If they must die because of their parents' sins, then they certainly "have no comforter." However, in actual fact the tears of these oppressed intercede for and protect the living, and because of their innocence and the power of their intercession a place is prepared for them to which even the perfectly righteous cannot attain or occupy; for the Holy One does in truth love them with a special and particular love. He unites himself with them and prepares for them a supernal place, very near to himself. It is concerning these that it is written: "Out of the mouth of babes and sucklings have You founded strength" (Psalm 8:2). (Zohar II, 113b)

Lurianic Kabbala

During the sixteenth century a settlement of kabbalists flourished in Safed in Galilee. For a time it centered about the great mystic genius Isaac Luria, who, building upon the imagery of the Zohar, developed several additional concepts that play a great role in Jewish mystical speculation. One of these is the concept of _simsum_ ("contraction"), which holds that since God fills all space, He had to contract Himself out of a minute portion of his infinity in order to make room for the created universe. Since this contraction took place equally on all sides, the resulting shape was spherical. The divine creative light entered into it in a straight line and arranged itself both in concentric circles and in a unilinear structure called "the Primordial Man that preceded all other primordials." The form of a circle and of a man are therefore the two directions in which every created thing develops.

Another concept developed in Lurianic kabbala is "the breaking of the vessels." The vessels assigned to the upper three _sefirot_ were able to contain the light that flowed into them, but the light struck the next six _sefirot_ all at once and so was too strong to be held by the individual vessels; one after another they broke, the pieces scattering and falling. The vessel of the last _sefira,_ Kingdom, also cracked but not to the same degree. Some of the light that had been in the vessels returned to its source, but the rest was hurled down with the vessels themselves and from these broken pieces the *kelippot,* the forces of darkness, took on strength. They are also the source of gross matter. The irresistible pressure of the light in the vessels also caused all the worlds to descend from the place that had been assigned to them, so the entire world process is at variance with its originally intended order and position.

The unfortunate effects of the breaking of the vessels can be overcome, Luria taught, by the process of *tikkun* ("restoration"). The chief agency of *tikkun* is the light that issued from Primordial Man's forehead to reorganize the confusion that resulted from the breaking of the vessels. Other complicated developments in which man can play no part have resulted in an almost complete achievement of the restoration, but there is yet work to be done, work that only man can do. It is the duty of the Jew through religious acts and mystic contemplation to struggle with and finally overcome the exile of his people, and also the exile of the Shekina caused by the breaking of the vessels. The Jew must work to restore the world to its true spiritual level and achieve a permanent state of communion between all creatures and God that the *kelippot,* the evil husks, will be unable to prevent.

Modern Philosophers

Moses Mendelssohn

The first Jewish philosopher in the modern era was Moses Mendelssohn who lived in the eighteenth century, the time of the German Enlightenment. He was a respected metaphysician and a pioneer in leading his fellow German Jews into participation in the secular culture of his time. (Although Sephardic Jews had often been involved in both the secular culture of the lands in which they lived and their own religious culture, this was by and large not true of Ashkenazic Jews before the late eighteenth century.) Many of the rabbis opposed secular learning. Mendelssohn led the

way into a new period in which German Jews for the first
time entered the professions, literature, and music. (Felix
Mendelssohn was his grandson.) Since many Jews could not
read the normal German letters Mendelssohn translated the
Torah into German written in Hebrew characters. This allowed Jews to use Mendelssohn's Bible for the purpose of
learning "correct" German speech in place of their own
Yiddish German dialect.

Mendelssohn's general philosophical writings demonstrate
that he partook generously in the intellectual spirit of his
time. Although he believed in the possibility of miracles, he
denied that they can be used to demonstrate the truth of any
one religion since all religions make claims to miraculous
events in the traditions they hand down. In reality, Mendelssohn said, basic religious truths are available to all humans and are not the product of supernatural revelation.
What is unique to the religion of the Jews is the revealed
legislation that is part of the Torah. Although Mendelssohn's ideas could not be considered orthodox in the conventional sense, he nonetheless remained an observant
Orthodox Jew throughout his life. He must be considered,
however, the spiritual ancestor of the various forms of non-
Orthodox Judaism that have come into being from the nineteenth century to the present day.

Mendelssohn's Jewish philosophic text is titled *Jerusalem*.
He writes there:

Judaism consisted—or according to the intention of the
founder, was to consist—first, of *religious doctrines and
tenets,* or eternal truths respecting God and his government and providence, without which man can be neither
enlightened nor happy. These were not forced upon the
belief of the people with threats of everlasting or tempo-
ral punishment, but rather, in conformity to the nature
and evidence of everlasting truths, were recommended to
their [the people's] rational acknowledgment and adoption. They needed not to be inspired into the people
through an immediate revelation, or made known through

word and writing, which are only intelligible on the spot
and at a given moment in time. The Most High Being has
revealed them to all rational creatures through fact and
mental conception, and written them in the soul with
such characters as are legible and intelligible at all times
and in all places. Their effect is as universal as the benefi-
cial influence of the sun who, while hastening through his
terrestrial course, diffuses light and warmth over the
whole terrestrial globe. As the prophet speaks in the
name of the Lord: "From the rising of the sun to his
setting, my name is known among the nations, and at
every place is incense burned to my name, and a pure
sacrifice is offered; for my name is great among the
nations."

Second, *Historical truths,* or accounts of the occur-
rences of ancient times, chiefly of the circumstances in
the lives of the progenitors of the Jewish people; of their
acknowledging the true God; of their walk before God;
even of their transgressions and the paternal chastisement which followed the same; of the covenant which
God established with them, and of the promise which He
often repeated to them, to raise up at some future day a
nation consecrated to his service out of their descendants. These historical accounts contained the foundation
of the national union; and as historical truths they can,
from their nature, not be received in any other manner
than upon belief. Authority alone gives them the evidence required; these accounts were also confirmed to
the nation by means of miracles, and supported by an
authority which was sufficient to place the belief beyond
all doubt and uncertainty.

Third, *Laws, ordinances, and commandments,* rules of
life that are peculiar to this people, and through the
observance of which they should not only reach national
prosperity, but every one of their members should also
attain to individual happiness. The Lawgiver was God;
not, indeed, in the relation of God the Creator and
Supporter of the universe, but as God the Suzerain and

Confederate of their forefathers, as Liberator, Founder and Leader, as King and Chief of this people; and He gave his laws the most solemn sanction, publicly and in a wonderful manner, such as never had been heard of, by which means they were rendered obligatory upon the nation and all their descendants, as their unalterable duty and obligation. (*Jerusalem,* p. 100)

Franz Rosenzweig

One of the influential Jewish thinkers of the twentieth century was Franz Rosenzweig, who died in 1929. The recipient of an excellent philosophical education in Germany, in his youth he was estranged from Judaism. In later years, though, he immersed himself in Jewish studies and set up centers of Jewish learning to attract German Jews to their faith. He also collaborated with Martin Buber on a translation of the Hebrew Scriptures into German.

Rosenzweig's philosophy of religion is contained in *The Star of Redemption.* Here he defines the three elements of existence as God, World, and Man. The paths linking these elements are Creation, Revelation, and Redemption. The elements can be considered as forming a triangle and the paths as forming a second triangle. When they are combined, they assume the shape of the six-pointed star, the symbol of Judaism. (This design, the so-called "Shield of David," came to be regarded as a uniquely Jewish symbol only in the late Middle Ages.) Rosenzweig asserts that the Bible partakes of divinity because, unlike the books of any of the eastern religions, it is rooted in the three paths and, even if all the claims of scientific biblical research should prove correct, it is still the only text that can inspire humanity toward correct religious insight. Both Judaism and Christianity originate in God, since they share a foundation in the Bible.

God as Redeemer is the consummation to which all true religion points.

Redemption has, as its final result, something which lifts it above and beyond the comparison with creation and revelation, namely God Himself. We have already said it: He is Redeemer in a much graver sense that He is Creator or Revealer. For He is not only the one who redeems, but also the one who is redeemed. In the redemption of the world by man, of man by means of the world, God redeems Himself. Man and world disappear in the redemption, but God perfects Himself. Only in redemption, God becomes the One and All which, from the first, human reason in its rashness has everywhere sought and everywhere asserted, and yet nowhere found because it simply was nowhere to be found yet, for it did not exist yet. We had intentionally broken up the All of the philosophers. Here in the blinding midnight sun of the consummated redemption it has at last, yea at the very last, coalesced into the One (*The Star of Redemption,* p. 238).

Rosenzweig was the first major Jewish philosopher to deal with the relationship of Christianity to Judaism in a serious way. He maintains that Judaism, the "star of redemption," is the eternal fire, while Christianity is the eternal rays that are emitted by that fire. The Jewish people, he says, stays with God, for it is the eternal people that has foresworn any portion in the world of pagan materiality. Christianity marches toward God, subduing the rest of the world for his sake.

The existence of the Jew constantly subjects Christianity to the idea that it is not attaining the goal, the truth, that it ever remains—on the way. That is the profoundest reason for the Christian hatred of the Jew, which is heir to the pagan hatred of the Jew. In the final analysis it is only self-hate, directed to the objectionable mute admonisher, for all that he but admonishes by his existence; it is hatred of one's own imperfection, one's own not-yet. By his inner unity, by the fact that in the narrowest confines of his Jewishness the Star of Redemption nonetheless still burns, the Jew involuntarily shames the Christian. (*The Star of Redemption*, p. 413).

Martin Buber

Martin Buber, who died in 1965, was born and educated in Germany, but he spent a number of years with his Hasidic grandfather in Poland, where he imbibed the traditions and "feel" of that mystical group within Judaism. (see p. 131.) During the last portion of his life, Buber lived in Jerusalem, where he was active in the pacifist cause and worked for mutual respect and understanding between Jews and Arabs.

He was the author of numerous books and articles, the most famous being *I and Thou*. There he expresses the hope that there might be less of the "I-It" relationship in human affairs, when people look upon each other as things to be analyzed and used, in the way of the scientist in the laboratory. Buber seeks more of the "I-Thou" relation, in which each person confronts his other as a totality, loving and accepting him in a deeply real but almost inexpressible manner. The I-Thou relation is manifest in the true appreciation of beauty; it is manifest in love, "ranging in its effect through the whole world. In the eyes of him who takes his stand in love and gazes out of it, men are cut free from their entanglement in bustling activity. Good people and evil, wise and foolish, beautiful and ugly, become successively real to him; that is, set free they step forth in their singleness and confront him as *Thou*." Buber said that it is the extended lines of I-Thou relationships that meet in the eternal Thou, God. "He who goes out with his whole being to meet his Thou and carries to it all being that is in the world, finds Him who cannot be sought." Organized religion, in its rites and its set forms of prayer, says Buber, results from the desire for an orderly and organized expression of the I-Thou relationship on the part of a community with its God.

Buber was opposed to the conventional type of mysticism

that seeks to withdraw from the world in order to achieve union with God. God is rather to be met by the one who goes his way within the world, simply wishing that it will be the right way. Regarding prayer Buber said, "The man who prays pours out himself in unrestrained dependence and knows that he has, in an incomprehensible way, an effect upon God, even though he obtains nothing from God; for when he no longer desires anything for himself he sees the flame of his effect burning at its height."

Shortly before his death Buber wrote the following:

> It is repugnant to me personally to wish to find the life substance of a community of faith like Judaism in a concept like "monotheism" that smacks so of an unbending world-view. But the belief in the Ehad (the One) I too hold to be the living center of Judaism. The confession of it expresses, indeed, two certainties in one: that of his uniqueness ("no other beside Him") and that of his unity (a being, a person, an eternal Thou). That the Jews living at any one time, those who are really Jews, thus confess themselves unreservedly to the Unique and the One, knowing with their whole soul that they are saying and answering for it with their whole lives, and that just these Jews from one time to another even so, with their whole souls and their whole lives, address Him, the unique and One, as their eternal Thou, in a community—"Our Father, our King"—and each alone—nothing else than Thou—that is the life-substance of Judaism. ("Replies to My Critics," *The Philosophy of Martin Buber,* edited by Schilpp and Friedman, p. 714)

Abraham Joshua Heschel

Although Martin Buber is the Jewish religious thinker of the twentieth century who had the largest following among Christian scholars in America and Western Europe, as well as among Jews who were interested in the subjects with which Buber was concerned, there was another Jewish philosopher who touched the hearts and minds of many people, both Jews and Christians. This was Abraham Joshua Heschel, who died in 1972 after a career as professor at the Jewish Theological Seminary in New York. Heschel grew up in Poland and was steeped in the tradition and lore of the Hasidim and Jewish mysticism. He took his university training in Germany and imbibed there the approach of scientific scholarship. His books are written in a simple, aphoristic style that still attracts many readers, even among the nonscholarly. Heschel sought through his writing to elucidate the spiritual quality of Judaism, rooted in a sense of awe for the presence of God, as well as the ethical message of the faith that is directed to all humanity.

In the pattern of his life Heschel exemplified the ideals about which he wrote. He was in the forefront of the American civil rights struggle as well as a public opponent of the war in Vietnam. He also played a major role as a consultant to the Vatican during the 1960s, while the Roman Catholic Church was developing its current views on Judaism and other religions and how these should be presented in the teachings of the Church.

Heschel maintained that the mystic experience is man's turning toward God, while the prophetic act is God's turning toward man. From the mystic experience we gain human insight into the life of God. Religion, he said, begins with God's question demanding man's answer, for God is in search of man to complete the work of creation, and He is involved in our destiny. From the work of the prophet, on the other hand, we partake of the insight of God into the life of humanity. "No one seems to hear the distress in the world. No one seems to care when the poor is suppressed. But God is distressed, and the prophet has pity for God who cares for the distressed." Our good deeds, Heschel says, are acts of communion with God. The destiny of man is to be a partner of God by fulfilling the *mitsvot* ("commandments").

Heschel wrote:

There is only one way to wisdom: awe. Forfeit your sense of awe, let your conceit diminish your ability to revere, and the universe becomes a marketplace for you. The loss of awe is the great block to insight. A return to reverence is the first prerequisite for a revival of wisdom, for the discovery of the world as an allusion to God. Wisdom comes from awe rather than from shrewdness. It is evoked not in moments of calculation but in moments of being in rapport with the mystery of reality. The greatest insights happen to us in moments of awe. A moment of awe is a moment of self-consecration. They who sense the wonder share in the wonder. They who keep holy the things that are holy shall themselves become holy. . . .

Where is the presence, where is the glory of God to be found? It is found in the world, in the Bible, and in a sacred deed. Do only the heavens declare the glory of God? It is deeply significant that Psalm 19 begins, "The heavens declare the glory of God," and concludes with a paean to the Torah and the *mitsvot*. The world, the word, as well as the sacred deed, are full of his glory. God is more immediately found in the Bible as well as in acts of kindness and worship than in the mountains and the forests. It is more meaningful for us to believe in the *immanence of God in deeds* than in the immanence of God in nature. Indeed, the concern of Judaism is primarily not how to find the presence of God in the world of things but how to let Him enter the ways in which we deal with things; how to be with Him in time, not only in space. This is why the *mitsva* ("commandment," "good deed") is a supreme source of religious insight and experience. The way to God is a way of God, and the *mitsva* is a way of God, a way where the self-evidence of the Holy is disclosed. We have few words, but we know how to live in deeds that express God. God is One, and his glory is One. And oneness means wholeness, indivisibility. His glory is not partly here and partly there; it is all here and all there. But here and now, in this world, the glory is concealed. It becomes revealed in a sacred deed, in a sacred moment, in a sacrificial deed. No one is lonely when doing a *mitsva,* for a *mitsva* is where God and man meet. (*God in Search of Man*, pp. 78, 311–312)

CHAPTER SEVEN

Modern Judaism

In Jewish teaching the Jewish people constitute a unity as descendants of the revered patriarchs whose sagas are told in the Scriptures. Most Jews do not think of themselves as "Orthodox" or "Reform"; they think of themselves simply as Jews. The Orthodox regard their practices and teachings as the only ones that are truly Jewish, but they do not deny the Jewish identity of people who participate in the other groups. (There is one exception to this principle: Many Orthodox do not accept the Jewish identity of converts who have been received into Judaism by non-Orthodox rabbis. They also deny the Jewish identity of the direct descendants of female converts who were received into Judaism by non-Orthodox rabbis. In order for such people to be accepted as Jews by Orthodoxy, they must undergo the conversion procedure under Orthodox auspices.) The majority of Jews, however, are neither converts nor the descendants of converts, so most Jews are able to think in terms of all Jews as "one people," and they are able to participate without qualm in the worship services of any branch of Judaism (although some Orthodox Jews will not go into a non-Orthodox synagogue for fear that their presence will be construed as giving approval to what is practiced and taught there). Many Jews who belong to a synagogue of a particular type in one community will gladly join a synagogue with another affiliation when they move to another community. And, except for some of the extremely rigid Orthodox, Jews of all persuasions are able to participate together in political and social causes and shared concerns. Marriage across denominational lines within Judaism is quite common; this in itself presents no problem unless there was a conversion in someone's ancestry that could be questioned by Orthodoxy.

Although most Jews subscribe to the conviction that they are one people, many who are active in the work and leadership structure of particular synagogues or religious movements take great pride in the institution that they support. While Orthodox Jews believe that their form of Judaism is the only valid and correct one, people who are active in Reform, Conservative, or Reconstructionist groups look upon their forms of Judaism as being best for them personally and for the community in which they participate. In an even more exaggerated way, most Hasidim regard the particular sect to which they belong as being "the best" and share pride and joy in being followers of the charismatic leader who heads their sect.

Viewed from a strictly logical perspective, there is probably more that divides the non-Orthodox Jew from the Orthodox than the teachings they share in common. From an emotional standpoint, however—and from the perspective of history—most Jews place an emphasis on what they share in common. Time will tell if this will continue to be the case or if the divisions within Judaism will become more divisive.

Orthodoxy

The body of Jews that remains faithful to the halaka—classical Jewish law as derived from the written Torah and the enactments of the rabbinic sages (the oral Torah)—is called "Orthodox." Orthodox Judaism remains committed to the idea that the written Torah was dictated by God verbatim to Moses and that the oral Torah is divinely inspired, all its teachings being implicit in the Torah of Moses and unfolding from generation to generation in the enactments and interpretations of the authentic teachers of Torah. In its theology Orthodoxy subscribes to the thirteen principles of Jewish faith enunciated by Maimonides (see p. 104), and to the belief that the Jews were exiled by God from the land of Israel because they did not live up to the commandments of the Torah. According to Orthodox thinking, when the Jewish people as a whole truly repents and commences to live in accordance with a proper understanding of the Torah, the Messiah will appear, the exile will be ended, the people will return to its true home, and the Temple will be rebuilt on the holy mount in Jerusalem.

It is understandable, given these commitments, that Orthodox Judaism is loath to permit changes in religious practice. It follows the principle, enunciated in the Talmud, that no body of rabbis can overturn the decision of a previous body of rabbis unless it is superior to its predecessor "in both wisdom and number." While it would always be possible to convene a body of rabbis superior in number to a predecessor body, it is by definition impossible to convoke a group that would be superior in wisdom to the sages of the past. It is axiomatic that the teachers of the past were wiser and more pious than those of the present; the farther one goes back into the past, the greater the wisdom that is attributed to its sages. Orthodoxy can only "change" an established religious practice handed down from the past if it can be shown that current conditions differ from those of the past and that the decision of the earlier sages was not meant to apply to these current conditions. Technically this is not a change, but rather the creation of new halaka to meet new conditions, deriving from the same interpretive process that the rabbis of the Talmud utilized in their day to define the authentic oral Torah. The process continues for all time, and no accepted decision of the past is ever "overturned."

Another reason for the reluctance of Orthodoxy to permit change in religious practice is that once a custom has become established, it assumes the status of law. Reverence must be shown to the customs followed by the people of the past. It is actually forbidden to "change the customs of our fathers" without weighty cause. (It should be noted, however, that Jews never adopted the approach of such groups as the Amish, who refuse to use electricity or automobiles. The acceptance of modern conveniences is not looked upon as a change of religious custom.) An example of a custom that assumed the status of law is the breaking of a glass at a Jewish wedding. Another is the requirement that Jewish men always keep their heads covered. This began as the personal practice of some of the scholars in Babylonia, who considered covering the head to be a sign of humility. It spread from them to the Jews of Spain and from there to other communities in Europe during the Middle Ages. It was never codified as a "law" in a technical sense, but it has become a practice so tenaciously cherished by Orthodox Judaism, and by many other Jews as well when praying or performing religious acts, that in popular thinking it is inseparable from Judaism. The skullcap (*yarmulke* in Yiddish, deriving from Latin *almucia; kippa* in Hebrew) played no religious role in biblical times or for many centuries thereafter, but by now its use is such a widespread custom that, in the estimation of many, it is a "sin" for a Jewish man to pray without one or, in certain Orthodox circles, to walk even a short distance without wearing one.

In the latter part of the twentieth century the wearing of the *yarmulke* has assumed an additional significance: it is a way of asserting a Jew's pride in his identity. A Jew who wears a *yarmulke* in the company of non-Jews thereby affirms his Jewishness and wishes those with whom he associates to accept and respect it. A religiously observant Jew who wears a *yarmulke* in the company of Jews who do not live by halaka affirms thereby his pride in the way of life, rooted in halaka, that he chooses to follow. The *yarmulke* also enables religious Jews to recognize each other as members of a common brotherhood within the anonymous mass of humanity.

The rules governing the observance of the Sabbath are, of course, more rigorous in Orthodox Judaism than in the other groups. Not only is "work" forbidden, but also many other acts that most people would not put in the category of work, such as writing or using the telephone. The purpose of these regulations is to set apart the Sabbath as a unique and holy day, one in which the joy of worship and study, as well as sharing hearty meals and religious song with other pious folk, will not be disturbed by the intrusions of every-day concerns. Travel by motor vehicle is forbidden, since this involves the kindling of fire for the engine to operate. Electricity may not be switched on for the same reason, but if a light was turned on before Friday sunset, when the Sabbath begins, its light may be enjoyed during the Sabbath. It may not be switched off until the Sabbath has ended, on Saturday at sunset. (However, automatic timing devices that do not involve human activity are acceptable to activate and turn off lights on the Sabbath.) Food may not be cooked, but it may be warmed on a stove whose flame was turned on before the Sabbath began. Buying and sell-ing, or any handling of money, are forbidden. In fact, carry-ing anything in one's hands or pockets is forbidden "in the public domain"—that is, outside the building or premises in which one happens to be. Carrying items, except those that may not be used on the Sabbath (such as money) is, how-ever, permissible "in the private domain." Orthodox fami-lies who live near one another may create their own private domain by establishing an *erub;* that is, they string a thin strand of wire to link their houses together and thereby create a private courtyard for halakic purposes, a space in which they may carry items back and forth or their children may play ball, and so forth. If the Orthodox Jews of an entire community agree, it is possible for such an *erub* to be established to cover a large geographic area. Even the most rigorous Orthodoxy, it should be noted, will set aside any of the Sabbath rules in an emergency that involves the saving of human life. The law stipulates that "the saving of life overrides the Sabbath," since Scripture long ago said that the laws of God were given that one might "live by them" (Leviticus 18:5) and not die.

Orthodox Judaism is very concerned about preserving the dietary restrictions of Jewish law. Only animals that are ritually fit (*kasher* or kosher) are acceptable for Jews to eat. For an animal to be kosher, it must have a split hoof and chew its cud. For sea creatures to be kosher, they must have both fins and scales. A kosher bird must not be a bird of prey. An animal that is acceptable for Jewish consumption must be slaughtered in the ritually correct manner. Milk or milk products must not be eaten at the same meal at which meat is eaten. Orthodox Jews usually have two complete sets of dishes: one for dairy products (including bread or cakes made with milk or butter) and the other for meat products. (The Orthodox Jew ordinarily has two additional sets of dishes as well, one for dairy foods during Passover and the other for meat foods during Passover.) Grains, vegetables, and fruits may be eaten with either meat or dairy foods. Some Orthodox Jews will eat only foods that are certified to be not just kosher but *glatt* kosher, a more stringent category which requires that the slaughtered animal be examined extremely closely for possible disqualification. When a *shohet* (ritual slaughterer) examines the lungs of a slaughtered animal and finds an imperfection, he attempts to remove the imperfection by touching it lightly with his finger. If this mark is easily removed, the animal is kosher. Ultra-Orthodox Jews, however, will not accept it, since they insist that there be no mark at all; the surface of the lung must be perfectly smooth (*glatt*). Stores or restaurants that sell *glatt* kosher food are under the supervision of an expert trained in the intricacies of the kosher laws, and they are forbidden to be open for business on the Sabbath.

The biblical laws dealing with foods that Jews may or may not eat are not accompanied by any explanations to support them. The rabbis in the Talmud expanded upon the biblical requirements (for instance in the regulations requiring different dishes for meat and dairy foods) in order to make a "fence," a protection about the biblical law so that it would be difficult for the people to inadvertently transgress. The dietary laws are not rationally explainable; they are decrees of the King, which his people are commanded to obey. They also serve the salutary purpose, from the standpoint of Orthodox Judaism, of reducing the opportunity for Orthodox Jews to socialize with non-Jews and with Jews who do not observe these rules. There is thus less chance that the observant Jew will find the nonobservant way of life attractive or be tempted to stray from his community and the practices that it enjoins. Consequently, an observant Orthodox Jew would be reluctant to attend a meeting or social gathering in a non-kosher restaurant, even though he would not be considered a "sinner" in the technical sense of the law unless he were to eat prohibited foods. Many Orthodox Jews in such a circumstance will content themselves with a cup of coffee or a glass of water to avoid using dishes that would not be kosher. Although the law in the Shulhan Aruk does not require this degree of meticulousness, few who are committed to Orthodoxy wish to deviate, even temporarily, from adherence to the law or give even the appearance of disregarding it. According to Orthodox halaka, one should not seem to disobey the law, even if one is observing it, because it would send the wrong message to the Jewish community and some people might be tempted to transgress. For the committed Orthodox Jew such things are not burdens to be borne with resignation. They are, rather, responsibilities to be accepted with joy, for the Jewish people are attendants upon the King of the universe, and this is the way of life that He has commanded them to live.

The worship services in Orthodox synagogues are in Hebrew. The sermon, if there is one, could be in English or any other language, and there might be some supplementary readings that are not in Hebrew. No organ or other instrumental music is played as part of a liturgical service. The prayer leader can be a layman or a *hazzan* with musical training, but he faces the Ark rather than the congregation and he is always a male. Choirs are allowed, although they, too, are all male.

Despite a popular misconception, Orthodox Judaism does not consider women inferior to men. It is incorrect to claim that this is the reason for the retiring role of women in the synagogue. The reason why women do not have leadership roles in the worship service is because they are not obligated to pray in the same way that men are, and only one who has an obligation to do something can, according to halaka, discharge that obligation for others. Women are not obligated to pray because it is assumed that they have responsibilities at home with children and other matters that will keep them away from the congregational gatherings. Men, on the other hand, can arrange their private affairs to be able to attend the services. In fact, women are obligated to observe only three positive ritual commandments that must be carried out at specified times: They must light and bless the Sabbath candles at sunset on Fridays; they must visit the ritual bath for purification each month seven days after menstrual flow has ceased, and, if they bake bread, they must throw a small piece of dough into the flames of the oven as a symbol of the offering that used to be given to the priests in Jerusalem. Women are seated in Orthodox synagogues in a section separate from the men for the same reason that they do not have leadership roles in the services. They are free to come and go as they wish, since they are not obligated to be there at all, according to halaka. Men, on the other hand, are obligated to be there and remain for the duration of the service. By having the women in an area separate from that of the men, the men's devotions will not be disturbed by the movements of the women. The women are often seated in a balcony area, but sometimes they remain on the same level as the men if a partition separates them.

Orthodox Judaism teaches that both men and women should dress and behave with proper modesty, although some groups of Orthodox are more concerned with this aspect of behavior than others. According to the more tradition-bound groups such as the Hasidim, women should not wear pants; their skirts and sleeves should be of proper length; and, if they are married, their hair should be covered by either a wig or a scarf. Except in rare circumstances, a married woman should not engage in extended conversation with a man who is not related to her. Men, too, are counseled not to have too much conversation with women or listen to a woman's singing. The clothing prescribed for both sexes should be of darkish color so as not to seem loud or immodest. The so-called "right wing Orthodox" groups are the ones who are vitally concerned with these matters. They also reject too much secular learning because it takes time away from religious texts. They segregate girls from boys in their schools even at a very young age, and they reject any kind of cooperation with Jewish groups that are not Orthodox. The so-called "modern Orthodox," on the other hand, encourage their children to receive a thorough secular education, sending them in many instances to non-Jewish universities; they do not necessarily segregate boys from girls in their schools; and they willingly join together with non-Orthodox Jews for discussion of communal concerns.

All Orthodox Jews are united in regarding homosexual behavior as a great sin, in rejecting the possibility of marriage between a Jew and a non-Jew who has not converted to Judaism, in rejecting the legitimacy of a marriage between a *kohen* of the priestly line of Aaron to a divorced woman or a convert to Judaism, and in insisting that Jewish identity can be transmitted to a child only through its mother.

In contemporary Orthodox Judaism there is little argument about either basic principles or the practices that the faith requires. This is because the authority of past tradition is decisive, and one who wishes to depart from the mandate of this authority realizes that he or she is no longer "orthodox" and really should belong to one of the other branches of Judaism. Thus, there are no Orthodox women who publicly agitate for the ordination of women as rabbis. Rabbis must be men, according to Orthodoxy, not because they are more intelligent than women but because from time to time they must participate in the judicial proceedings of rabbinic courts or act as witnesses before such courts. Women, according to halaka, are not allowed to function as witnesses since many of them (although not all) would be too prone to emotion to be able to operate in such a setting on a strictly dispassionate basis. Halaka legislates with the majority in mind rather than the exceptional few; so, while some women can be fine scholars, the rabbinical office, with its communal responsibilities, is not open to them. Likewise, there are no Orthodox women demanding that they be allowed to lead worship services for men, because they know that halaka long ago ruled against such a possibility. What some contemporary women do seek is the right to conduct services for groups made up exclusively of women. Some of the "modern Orthodox" authorities are willing to allow this, but the "right-wing Orthodox" will not, since they fear that it would open the door to further deviations from accepted practice. Besides, the feminist movement seeking wider participation by women in functions traditionally reserved for men is inspired by non-Jewish and secular example, and halaka forbids the adoption of non-Jewish practices in the realm of religion.

Hasidism

Among the groups that make up Orthodox Judaism are the various sects of the Hasidim ("pious ones"). Hasidism took form in Poland during the eighteenth century as the creation of Israel son of Eliezer, known as the Baal Shem Tob ("the Master of the Good Name"). It took root among Jews who had been impoverished by the Ukrainian revolt and attendant massacres during the seventeenth century, as well as by the subsequent disillusionment that followed after the collapse of the messianic movement centered upon Sabbetai Sebi. (See p. 199) Within the Jewish community itself the needs of the poor were ill-served by many in the scholar class, who held themselves aloof from them and equated piety with the mastery of abstruse halakic arguments in complicated texts. The Baal Shem Tob came to the Jews of the Carpathian region of Poland not with a message of revolt against halaka (he was devoted to the observance of both biblical and rabbinic law, and he urged his followers to stay faithful to the tradition); he came, rather, with a new spirit and attitude that he was able to infuse into his "hasidim," one which enabled them to surmount the poverty and pain in which many existed. Unlike many of the scholars for whom prayer and religious observance were solemn matters indeed, the Baal Shem taught that God pays heed to worship only when it is offered in joy. Song and dance should accompany prayer, for true piety exists only when one is exhilarated by the sense of God's presence. The Baal Shem was very much influenced by Lurianic kabbala; in fact, Hasidism might be called a populist version of the Jewish mystical tradition. Instead of remaining the province of a few esoteric specialists, the mystical concern to hasten the time of redemption became a responsibility of ordinary people as well. Key concepts in Hasidic practice are "concentration" (*kavvana*), "enthusiasm," and "cleaving to God." Many ritual acts are accompanied by the recitation of Luria's formula: "Behold I am ready and prepared to fulfill this commandment for the sake of uniting the Holy One blessed be He with his Shekina, through the means of this concealed mystery, in the name of all Israel."

Hasidism spread, despite much opposition from other Jews, through wide regions of Poland, the Ukraine, White Russia, Romania, and Hungary. In addition to the enthusiasm of Hasidic worship that distinguishes it from the practice of other Orthodox Jews, many Hasidim are unique in retaining the style of dress, particularly on Sabbath and holy days, that was worn by their ancestors in the eighteenth century. The men wear black suits and hats, and most refuse ties. On Sabbaths, some Hasidic men put on the round fur hat, the *streimel,* and the long silk coat, the *kapote,* in honor of the day. In this way the Hasidim not only observe the Jewish tradition that emphasizes modesty in dress and behavior, but also demonstrate their love and reverence for the ancestors who dressed in this way. Most importantly, however, Hasidic men follow literally the injunction of Numbers 15:39, requiring that fringes be placed upon the corners of their garments so that they might look upon them and be reminded of God's commandments. Other Orthodox Jews wear the fringes under their clothing, but Hasidim take out the four fringes (two in front and two in back) and let them hang out over their trousers in order that they might see them as the Bible prescribes. Hasidim also take pride in the commandment of Leviticus 19:27, "You shall not trim the hair on your temples or mar the corners of your beard." Other Orthodox Jews, following Mishna Makkot 3:5, interpret this to mean that a straight razor should not be used to shave the beard, but an electric razor or a depilatory is acceptable. Hasidim, however, take the verse literally and consider it a religious obligation to grow both beard and side-curls. Some of them cultivate extremely long side-curls, which eventually have to be placed behind the ears for safety's sake. They seek in this way to affirm publicly their Jewishness and the joy that they feel in living in accordance with God's word.

Women in Hasidic communities are expected, above all, to exhibit modest and chaste behavior at all times. Their sleeves should reach the wrist and their skirts extend almost to the ankle. If married, they should cover their hair when outside their own home. Arranged marriages are quite common among Hasidim, and very often the approval of the *rebbe*, the leader of a Hasidic group, will be sought before a marriage can take place. Most Hasidim do not watch television or go to theaters because the behavior portrayed there is so much at variance with the ideals by which they live.

The Hasidim after the time of the Baal Shem Tob came to revere various charismatic leaders whom they styled "rebbes" (derived from *rabbi*). A number of them were reputed to have miracle-working powers. Hasidim ordinarily attach themselves to one particular rebbe to whom they look for guidance in all areas of life. A Hasid seeks to be in the presence of his rebbe whenever possible, for the rebbe is close to God and can transmit some of the power and holiness that he possesses to those who love and follow him.

Over the years the groups that coalesced about particular rebbes came to constitute distinct sects centered about specific locations in Eastern Europe where the rebbes held court. Many of these groups are now represented in Israel and the United States, and in lesser numbers in Western Europe and Latin America. Some sects feel a sense of rivalry with other sects, while others seek to cultivate attitudes of mutual respect toward other Hasidic groups (and other Orthodox Jews as well). Hasidim have increased in both numbers and significance in many Jewish communities because they function with a great degree of cohesiveness and very often have a high birth rate, following closely the commandment of the Torah to "be fruitful and multiply."

Some of the major Hasidic groups flourishing today are those of Bratslav, Belz, Bobov, Ger, Radzyn, Lubavitch, and Satmar. The Satmar Hasidim are known far and wide for their antipathy toward the State of Israel. The Lubavitcher Hasidim (known also as *Habad,* an acronym from the Hebrew words for "wisdom," "understanding," and "knowledge") are, on the other hand, passionately devoted to the State of Israel and its welfare and have established institutions over the entire world seeking to lead Jews of all kinds to an appreciation of the faith and its traditions. Many of the Lubavitchers are convinced that when at last the Messiah will come, it will be their rebbe who will fill that role in God's plan.

Reform

The work of Moses Mendelssohn inspired many Jews living in Central Europe in the late eighteenth century to immerse themselves in the culture, including the literature and science, of the German-speaking lands in which they lived. Subsequently, the French Revolution and the armies of Napoleon carried democratic ideals into these regions, and it was not long thereafter that a number of Jews decided that, in the new world that was coming into being, a "reform" of some Jewish practices was in order. The Reform movement began at first with slight changes in the worship services (for example, seeking to eliminate repetition and provide for better order and decorum within the congregations), but ideological changes were not far behind as rabbis who were also trained in scientific historical method became involved. The aim of the Reform movement was to retain for Judaism people who sought a more modern and rationalistic approach and who no longer found meaning or inspiration in the old patterns of practice and belief. Large numbers of people from Germany and other areas of Central Europe migrated to the United States during the mid-nineteenth century; among them were Jews who found the spirit of Reform congenial to their needs. Thus it was that Reform Judaism came to be the dominant expression of the faith in many American communities for quite some time. Its seminary, the Hebrew Union College in Cincinnati, was established in 1875.

The Reform movement eliminated separate seating for men and women in the synagogue service, shortened the prayers, and authorized many of the readings to be done in the vernacular of the country rather than in Hebrew. Mixed choirs of men and women were organized for the musical portions of the liturgy, and organ or other instrumental accompaniment was encouraged. The need for special ritual dress for Jews, including the knotted fringes and the skullcap or other head covering, was eliminated, as were the dietary restrictions. The rules governing Sabbath observance were relaxed, so that the use of electricity and automobiles on that day became legitimate. The Reformers denied the old belief in the bodily resurrection of the dead at the end of days, and they changed the expectation of a messianic king of the line of David to a hope that a "messianic age" would come to fruition, when peace and human brotherhood would be the rule rather than the exception. The belief in a Messiah had developed when kings and emperors held sway, so it was logical for the hope to grow that, as part of the redemption, a totally righteous king would rule the world.

But when Reform Judaism was taking form democracy was in the process of replacing monarchy, and the idea of a Messiah who would be "king of the world" had much less appeal than in the past.

The changes made by Reform Judaism in both religious practice and belief were rooted in a basically scientific attitude toward both Scripture and the oral Torah. Although some of the first Reformers believed in the divine origin of the Torah, modern biblical study became part of the Reform rabbinic curriculum, and the doctrine of "progressive revelation" came to replace the belief that God had revealed Himself for all time to Moses. The doctrine of the "mission of Israel," the idea that the Jews had been sent to all the corners of the earth to share the concepts of "ethical monotheism" with all peoples replaced the traditional conviction that the Jews had been exiled from their ancient homeland because of sin. The Reformers were convinced that it would not be long before a rational, democratic monotheistic faith, rooted in the teachings of the biblical prophets, would become the heritage of all humanity and that the Jewish people as a whole, once the process of Reform was complete, would be the apostles of that faith. Many of the Reform rabbis in America equated the democratic and egalitarian ideals of the Declaration of Independence, the Constitution, and the Bill of Rights with the teachings of Reform Judaism.

The rabbis of American Reform Judaism expressed their philosophy in the Pittsburgh Platform of 1885 in the following way:

> We recognize in the Bible the record of the consecration of the Jewish people to its mission as priest of the one God, and value it as the most potent instrument of religious and moral instruction. We hold that the modern discoveries of scientific researches in the domains of nature and history are not antagonistic to the doctrines of Judaism, the Bible reflecting the primitive ideas of its own age, and at times clothing its conception of Divine

Providence and justice dealing with man in miraculous narratives. We recognize in the Mosaic legislation a system of training the Jewish people for its mission during its national life in Palestine, and today we accept as binding only the moral laws, and maintain only such ceremonies as elevate and sanctify our lives, but reject all such as are not adapted to the views and habits of modern civilization. . . . We recognize, in the modern era of universal culture of heart and intellect, the approaching of the realization of Israel's great messianic hope for the establishment of the kingdom of truth, justice, and peace among all men. We consider ourselves no longer a nation, but a religious community, and therefore expect neither a return to Palestine, nor a sacrificial worship under the sons of Aaron, nor the restoration of any of the laws concerning the Jewish state.

Over the years it became quite clear that the lofty hopes of Reform Judaism for the world were not going to be soon realized. The advent of Nazism in Germany demonstrated that a vicious anti-Semitism persisted and that the position of Jews in a society could be very precarious indeed. In addition, in North America, the seat of the Reform movement, the demographics of the Reform Jewish community began to change. Though originally a movement made up almost exclusively of people of German or other Central European backgrounds who were comfortable with a rationalist and nonritualistic approach, Reform temples in the twentieth century began to attract more and more congregants of East European derivation who wanted more ritual in the service, including a return to the use of Hebrew, and who did not reject either Zionism or the national and ethnic basis inherent in Judaism itself. For this reason the Reform rabbis in 1937 promulgated the Columbus Platform, slightly changing the orientation of the movement:

Judaism is the historical religious experience of the Jewish people. Though growing out of Jewish life, its message is universal, aiming at the union and perfection of mankind under the sovereignty of God. . . . The Torah, both written and oral, enshrines Israel's ever-growing consciousness of God and of the moral law. It preserves the historical precedents, sanctions, and norms of Jewish life and seeks to mold it in the patterns of goodness and of holiness. . . . Judaism is the soul of which Israel is the body. Living in all parts of the world, Israel has been held together by the tie of a common history, and above all, by the heritage of faith. . . . In all lands where our people live, they assume and seek to share loyally the full duties and responsibilities of citizenship and to create seats of Jewish knowledge and religion. In the rehabilitation of Palestine, the land hallowed by memories and hopes, we behold the promise of renewed life for many of our brethren. We affirm the obligation of all Jewry to aid in its upbuilding as a Jewish homeland by endeavoring to make it not only a haven of refuge for the oppressed but also a center of Jewish culture and spiritual life. . . . Judaism as a way of life requires in addition to its moral and spiritual demands the preservation of the Sabbath, festivals, and Holy Days; the retention and development of such customs, symbols, and ceremonies as possess inspirational value; the cultivation of distinctive forms of religious art and music; and the use of Hebrew, together with the vernacular, in our worship and instruction.

In addition to its bastion in the United States and Canada, Reform Judaism is present in Israel, Great Britain, France, South Africa, Australia, and several countries in Latin America. For the most part, Reform Jews are rather secular people whose way of life is quite different from that of committed Orthodox Jews. Their way of life is nearly indistinguishable from that of many liberal Christians or other moral people who may not have any religious affiliation. In spite of this, however, the dedicated Reform Jew is conscious and proud of his tie to the past of his people and seeks through learning and good works to transmit this heritage to his children. Many of them are convinced that Reform Judaism, more emphatically than any other segment within the Jewish religious community, best preserves the heritage of "prophetic Judaism." That is to say, Reform Judaism, like the prophets of the Bible, teaches the primacy of ethics and the responsibility of humanity to formulate a more wholesome and equitable society. Purely ritualistic behavior is of decidedly secondary importance in the face of this overwhelming moral imperative.

Though there is a small group of rabbis within the movements who lead congregations dedicated to "humanistic Judaism" and are convinced that the word *God* possesses no self-evident meaning and should therefore no longer be used, the sense of God's presence is a reality to most Reform Jews. One of the best-loved prayers in the Reform liturgy is the following:

> Grant us peace, your most precious gift, O Eternal Source of peace, and give us the will to proclaim its message to all the peoples of the earth. Bless our country that it may always be a stronghold of peace and its advocate among the nations. May contentment reign within its borders, health and happiness within its homes. Strengthen the bonds of friendship among the inhabitants of all lands, and may the love of your name hallow every home and every heart. Blessed is the Eternal God, the Source of peace.

In response to contemporary feminism, Reform Judaism has opened its rabbinical and cantorial schools to women. The first woman was ordained a rabbi in 1972. Recognizing that homosexuality may be an innate condition rather than a matter of deliberate choice, the movement has gone on record in recent years to welcome homosexuals into its temples and has allowed the affiliation of temples with a primarily homosexual outreach, provided that non-homosexuals are eligible for membership as well.

With regard to the vexing question of whether Reform rabbis should officiate at the marriage of a Jew to someone who is not Jewish and has no wish to convert to Judaism, the movement has always been on record as opposing such officiation. However, rabbis have always had the freedom to interpret ritualistic matters as they see fit, so a large percentage of Reform rabbis have eschewed the official recommendation and are willing to officiate at these marriages, provided their own individual requirements are satisfied by the couples involved. Since the rate of Jewish intermarriage with non-Jews approaches 50 percent in many communities, the question is of great importance to both rabbis and others. Although Orthodox halaka denies Jewish identity to the children of non-Jewish mothers who have not converted to Judaism before giving birth, Reform practice has been to affirm the Jewishness of these children if their parents raise them within Judaism. As a result of the publicity given in recent years to this practice in response to the rising rate of intermarriage, Orthodox authorities have taken to denouncing Reform Judaism with renewed vehemence. Many Conservative leaders oppose this policy, too.

Conservatism

Conservative Judaism may well be the most populous of the organized Jewish groups in the United States (although the number of Jews who are unaffiliated with any form of Judaism may be the largest of all). The movement is indigenously American, beginning as a reaction against the 1885 Pittsburgh Platform on the part of rabbis and scholars who were more "conservative" in their approach. They drew their inspiration from the example of earlier scholars in Germany who believed that Judaism should be studied in accordance with historical principles but who felt that many of the "radical reformers" had gone too far in their modifications of Jewish practice. Shortly after the founding of the movement's rabbinic academy, the Jewish Theological Seminary in New York, a group of wealthy Reform Jews gave it generous financial support and continued to do so over many years, for they felt that it had the potential to acculturate and "Americanize" the millions of East European Jews who were migrating to the United States during the early part of the twentieth century. These philanthropists realized that these immigrants would not be comfortable in the Germanic Reform temples of the time; the nascent Conservative movement offered them the kind of Judaism that they needed, one that blended American values with the ritual and warm feeling that they associated with being Jewish.

In its early days Conservative Judaism was indistinguishable from Orthodoxy. Its synagogue services utilized the Orthodox Siddur, the men were separated from the women, and the prayer leader faced the Ark rather than the congregation. The only unique aspect of Conservative services was that there would usually be an English sermon, there might be some English supplementary readings in which the congregation participated, and the "decorum" of the worshippers would be more restrained or "dignified" than in some Orthodox synagogues, where it is not unknown for people to pray individually at their own speed, walk in and out of the room, or occasionally converse with a neighboring worshipper. Nothing that the Conservative groups instituted in these early days contravened halaka; the movement functioned as a more "Americanized" version of Orthodoxy. This state of affairs was not to last, however. There emerged a fairly small group of "left-wing Conservatives" who installed organs in their synagogues and had them played to accompany Sabbath and holy day worship. According to some interpreters, this does not go against halaka if the organist is not Jewish, since only Jews are prohibited from playing musical instruments on the Sabbath. According to others, though, the use of the organ in the synagogue is prohibited by halaka because it is in imitation of non-Jewish practice. The answer of those who advocate the organ is that its use is not in imitation of what non-Jews do at their religious services, but rather an adaptation of what contemporary Jews are doing at Reform temples. The stricter interpreters are not impressed by these arguments because the practice is, in any event, a "change of the custom of our ancestors" and is likely to lead to other even more improper changes in liturgical practice. Even though only a small minority of Conservative synagogues uses organs or other musical instruments at worship services, the fact that such a thing is tolerated by the movement in itself constituted a breach with Orthodoxy.

A more egregious breach with Orthodoxy occurred when the Conservative movement countenanced the mixed seating of men and women at worship services. This without any question contravenes halakic practice. Conservative Judaism acted in response to the demands of the many women who were among the most dedicated workers on behalf of their synagogues, but who nonetheless were prohibited from sitting with their husbands at worship services. Orthodox Judaism found it impossible, after the authorization of mixed seating by the Conservative movement, to accept the religious legitimacy of such a decision, and the separation between the two Jewish groups was complete. Later on, Conservatism authorized the counting of women as part of the *minyan,* the required quorum of ten for worship services, as well as the calling of women from the congregation to recite the blessings at the reading of the Torah. (Not all Conservative synagogues or rabbis allow these practices, but the number that does so is increasing with time.) It was not until 1985 that the last barrier to women's full participation in religious life fell within the Conservative movement. This occurred when the first woman was ordained a rabbi. A caucus of traditionalist Conservative rabbis was formed to combat this development. The group still exists, seeking to prevent further defections from halakic precedent, but its members have not withdrawn from the Conservative fellowship.

Conservative Judaism also took major steps to liberalize the rules governing Sabbath observance. One decision authorized the use of a motor vehicle in order to attend or return from the synagogue on the Sabbath. (In theory, other uses of an automobile on the Sabbath, except to save life, are still prohibited to Conservative Jews.) Also, the use of certain electrical appliances in the home, including the telephone, radio, and television, was authorized on the Sabbath if and when the purpose is to enhance the enjoyment and appreciation of the Sabbath. The responsum declares,

> In the use of radio or television common sense should dictate that only such programs may be indulged which are not vulgar and banal and do not desecrate the sanctity of the ideal Sabbath. Only programs of high esthetic taste, of high ethical content, instructive, and of social value are in keeping with our concept of Sabbath holiness and only such programs should be listened to and seen on the Sabbath day.

Conservative Jews are expected to observe the dietary restrictions of Jewish tradition, but, of course, most are not as strict as truly Orthodox Jews would be. While an Orthodox Jew would likely not eat any cooked food or even bread in a non-kosher restaurant, a Conservative Jew would abstain from meat dishes or at least the meat of animals prohibited by the Torah but would in all likelihood be willing to eat anything else. While an Orthodox Jew would be expected to wear a *yarmulke* or other head covering at all times, a Conservative Jew would likely do so only when at worship or while reading a sacred Hebrew text.

Conservative Judaism's great success has been based upon its adoption of the middle way between Orthodoxy and Reform. In recent years, however, the way of life of most Conservative Jews has been gravitating toward that of most Reform Jews. Although the dietary laws, for instance, are of great importance in Conservative teaching, many Conservative Jews ignore these regulations to a greater or lesser degree. Reform Judaism is moving toward more ritual practice in its synagogue services and in the observance of the holy days, while segments of Orthodoxy have become extremely militant in denouncing Conservatism as an even greater threat to true Judaism than Reform. What is developing today, therefore, is a closer coalescence of the three non-Orthodox branches of Judaism—Reform, Conservative, and Reconstructionist—in areas of ritual practice and even in ideology. As time goes on the lines separating these groups should become even more indistinct, and American Judaism will, for all essential purposes, be divided into two camps—the Orthodox and the non-Orthodox. Only time will tell which camp will ultimately win the allegiance of that portion of the Jewish community that desires to label itself in terms of religious inclination.

The major area in which differences still exist between Conservative and Reform Judaism is that of "personal status." Reform allows its rabbis who wish to do so to officiate at the marriage of Jews to non-Jews, while Conservatism does not; Reform regards as Jews the children of non-Jewish mothers who are raised as Jews, but Conservatism does not. In Israel, where these differences do not exist between the two groups, the small Reform and Conservative communities are for all practical purposes united.

Reconstructionism

The Reconstructionist movement was founded by Mordecai Kaplan, who died in 1983 at the age of 102. Kaplan taught for many years at the Jewish Theological Seminary, the academy of Conservative Judaism. Reconstructionism has relatively recently structured itself as one of the four major divisions within American Judaism (its own seminary was founded in Philadelphia in 1968), but for most of its existence it sought to function as a force and influence within the three other branches of the faith. Even today some would define Reconstructionism as "left-wing Conservatism."

Reform and Conservative rabbis, and even some "modern Orthodox," have all been influenced by Kaplan's ideas. The seminal publication in which he expounded his philosophy is *Judaism as a Civilization*, which was published in 1934. Kaplan was heavily influenced by the pragmatic philosophy of John Dewey, an approach that does not seek after universally valid absolute truths, but rather after that which works and produces good results in human society. Kaplan emphasized the peoplehood of all Jews regardless of the theological beliefs to which individuals or groups might subscribe and the consequent necessity for an organized Jewish community life. He regarded Judaism as the primary folk expression of the Jewish people. This is the source of the vitality of the Jewish religion, rather than any commitment to its divine origin. It provides a meaningful world in which Jews can function, even those who would not be considered "religious" in a traditional sense. Religion is essentially a healthy reaction to life, containing emotional, volitional, and intellectual elements. Jewish laws and customs are "folkways" that should be preserved as much as possible because they express the concept of Jewish peoplehood in a dramatic way. In the prayerbook that he edited Kaplan did away with any reference to the Jews as a "chosen people," believing that it was not God but rather the national culture of the Jewish people that predisposed it toward spirituality and ethical principles. God for Kaplan is a Power in the universe sympathetic to humanity; God is Process, particularly social process, making for righteousness and a meaningful life.

Kaplan wrote:

> It is one thing to identify and name the factors which condition the conception of God—fear, ghosts, animism, the yearning for protection; it is quite another to infer that the conception of God can be resolved entirely into the factors which condition it. The inference which reduces the God-idea to an illusion is not logically justified by the psychologic data of religion, but derives rather from an antipathy to religion. Psychologists who reduce the God-idea to an illusion disregard the changing character of the God-idea. They usually attack an outgrown God-idea,

and overlook the fact which might have served at least as a psychologic datum, that as soon as one God-idea is discarded, another one, which is regarded as a closer approximation to the truth, emerges. They also forget that the very condemnation of an idea as illusory implies the existence of some reality which is regarded as the norm. Why may not the quality of godhood reside in that very reality which serves as a criterion for rejecting as illusions the traditional or conventional ideas of God? (*Judaism as a Civilization*, p. 309).

In the years after the founding of the Reconstructionist Seminary, people who were interested in exploring new forms of Jewish spiritual expression began to gravitate to it, both as faculty and students. Some were radical feminists, others were interested in adapting aspects of Hasidic prayer and meditation to the framework of a liberal form of Judaism. Some were pacifists of varying degrees, or vegetarians. Many like to use the term "new age" to describe their approach to Judaism and life in general. It remains to be seen if the Reconstructionist movement will integrate some of these causes into itself and thus move them into the mainstream of contemporary Jewish life.

Zionism and the State of Israel

Traditional Jewish law stipulates that a Jew should, if at all possible, settle in the land of Israel. Many Jews over the centuries have done so. For the most part they were Orthodox Jews acting in response to the recommendation of the halaka; many of them came to the Holy Land for the express purpose of dying there and being buried in the sacred soil. During the last quarter of the nineteenth century, however, a new type of movement centering about the resettlement of Jews in the land of Israel took shape in Eastern Europe. The pogroms and persecutions in the Russian Empire led many Jews to emigrate to America, but another group saw the salvation of the people in a return to the ancient homeland, where they could become "pioneers" on the land, working as farmers like their ancestors thousands of years ago. Small groups went by land or by sea to Palestine and attempted to fulfill their dream. Many of the Orthodox authorities objected to what they thought was an arrogant preemption of the role of the Messiah who, they said, was to lead the Jews back to their land in God's good time, but others supported the efforts of the pioneers.

During the 1890s a Viennese journalist, Theodor Herzl, was sent to Paris to cover the "Dreyfus affair," the trial and conviction of a Jewish military officer accused of spying against his country. The verdict had been obtained on the basis of forged evidence, and Dreyfus was eventually exonerated. France, however, was racked for years with impassioned debate between those who saw him as innocent and those who saw him as guilty (or who preferred that the guilty verdict not be set aside even if it could not be proven). Herzl, a nonreligious Jew, was shocked by the vicious antiSemitism of many anti-Dreyfusards; this, after all, was France, the birthplace of liberty and equality. He became convinced that there could be no liberty or equality for Jews except in their own land. Thus, Herzl founded the Zionist movement, an organization devoted to pleading the cause of a Jewish state in Palestine, then under Turkish rule, before the crowned heads and other rulers of Europe. Herzl died in 1904, but he predicted that within fifty years the Jewish state would be a reality. During World War I Great Britain issued a document supporting the concept of Palestine as a Jewish national homeland. Then, after conquering the area from the Turks, Britain was entrusted with a mandate over the territory by the League of Nations. The Zionist organization sought to encourage Jewish settlement in Palestine, and many responded to the call—but not enough; in theory, the Holocaust of the Jews of Europe during World War II could have been averted if sufficient numbers had settled in Palestine earlier.

The Zionist movement became a coalition of various parties, reflecting the political composition of the Jewish community in Palestine. There were centrist groups, socialist parties, and those representing the goals of the "religious," that is, the Orthodox. The Revisionist group, the forerunner of the Likud party in today's Israel, was a militant right-wing faction that remained apart from the general Zionist coalition; it sought a Jewish state that would encompass the land on both sides of the Jordan River. There was also a very small Unity group that advocated a binational state in which both Jews and Arabs, together with their respective cultures, would be absolutely coequal, but few people paid much attention to this alternative. The Arabs, who had rioted against Jewish settlement since the 1920s, wanted only a token number of Jews in what they considered "their" land, while the Jews, of course, wanted a state of their own. Besides, most Jews looked upon most Arabs as fairly primitive people, who would constitute no great threat in the long run; if they did not like the idea of living in a Jewish state, Jews contended, Arabs could always move to one of the neighboring Arab lands. The Jews of the United States were for the most part sympathetic to Zionism, but few of them wished to go to Palestine. Within the Reform group a number of rabbis and laymen were opposed in principle to a Jewish state, since they felt that it would endanger the position of Jews in other countries who might be accused of "dual loyalty." Other Reform rabbis, as well as the great majority of Conservative and Orthodox rabbis, were supporters of Zionism. Practically all the lay people in the Conservative movement were strongly pro-Zionist.

In 1947 Great Britain informed the United Nations that it wished to surrender its mandate over Palestine. After months of hearings and diplomatic activity, the United Nations voted to partition Palestine into separate Jewish and Arab states, with Jerusalem itself to be under international jurisdiction. The Arab nations refused to accept this decision by the United Nations, and five of them sent troops into Palestine as soon as the British mandate ended. Despite opposition from within and without, the Jewish leadership proclaimed the birth of the State of Israel at the termination of British sovereignty on May 14, 1948. Israeli forces were able to defeat the Arab armies, and Israel found itself in control of even more territory than had been allotted to it in the United Nations partition plan. It was also able to occupy much of Jerusalem, though not the Old City with its sacred sites. The Old City, together with predominantly Arab territory that came to be called the West Bank, was in the hands of forces from Jordan. Jews, as well as others who were sympathetic to the Zionist cause, had come from all over the world to aid Israel in its war of independence, and their cause had been successful. The State of Israel opened its gates to the thousands of Jews in Europe who had been rescued from the death camps of the Holocaust at the end of World War II and had remained in limbo as "displaced persons" since 1945. Israel also opened its doors to thousands of Jews forced to leave Arab lands after the fury of murderous mobs had been turned against them in revenge for the emergence of Israel.

Once the State of Israel came into existence, practically all organized opposition to Zionism disappeared within the Jewish communities of America and Western Europe. The exception is the Satmar Hasidim and a few other "right-wing Orthodox" who oppose a Jewish state in the absence of the Messiah and object moreover that this state, which they say should not exist, is not governed solely by Torah law. The old Reform opposition to Zionism lives on not in the form of opposition to the State of Israel, a foreign country about which Americans need not necessarily be concerned, but in the form of opposition to the ritualism and use of Hebrew, allegedly influenced by Israel, that has become so prominent in contemporary Reform Judaism. American Jews have become conditioned to support Israel through the United Jewish Appeal, contributions to which support a number of public and private charitable projects in Israel, and through the purchase of Israel Bonds.

In 1967 Israel launched a preemptive strike against Egypt, which had been planning an attack. Israeli forces were able to occupy the Sinai peninsula and also wrest the West Bank and the Old City of Jerusalem from Jordan, which had moved against Israel in support of Egypt. The conflict ended in six days' time. Jerusalem was rejoined to that portion of the city that Israel already possessed, and it was annexed to Israel proper as the "eternal capital" of the state. In 1973 Egypt moved against Israeli forces in the Sinai; this time the outcome was not as conclusive as in past conflicts, and the United States negotiated a disengagement of forces between the two opposing sides. Arab "honor" had been vindicated, since Egypt had been able to repel an Israeli advance into its territory, and in 1977 President Sadat of Egypt offered to visit Jerusalem for negotiations with Israeli leaders. As a result of that historic meeting, the United States was able to broker the Camp David agreements and an Israeli-Egyptian peace treaty. The Sinai was returned to Egypt, and Israel undertook, in conjunction with the United States and Egypt (and Jordan as well if it wished to participate) to negotiate a period of "autonomy" for the Arabs of the West Bank, following which there would be a final determination of the status of that territory. The Israelis were deliberately vague about what they meant by "autonomy," so this provision of the treaty was never implemented.

During the years that Israel was developing its sense of nationhood, the Palestinian Arabs were also developing a much stronger national identity than they had possessed before. Thousands of Arab Palestinians had fled the territory that became Israel in 1948 to neighboring Arab countries, where they and their children and grandchildren sat and remembered the land they had left behind. In time, a number of Palestinian organizations took form that were dedicated to the eradication of the "Zionist entity" from Arab soil. These came together in 1964 as the Palestine Liberation Organization (the PLO). Over the years the PLO has sponsored terrorist attacks against Israel and Israelis, and Israel has responded with air attacks and other forms of retaliation against PLO entrenchments wherever they might be. Beginning in 1987 Palestinian teenagers living on the

West Bank (and in Gaza, the other heavily Arab district occupied by Israel in 1967) initiated the *intifada*, a small-scale uprising against Israeli forces to protest the occupation of their land that seems to have no end in sight. Although many Israelis are willing to concede occupation of the West Bank, some of the Orthodox and right wing factions are not, maintaining that it is part of the God-given heritage of the Jewish people. (Quite a few Orthodox settlements have been established on the West Bank.) The leadership of the PLO, meanwhile, has moderated its position, with many in the PLO now willing to accept an Israeli state next to a Palestinian state. However, the current Israeli leadership seems unwilling to accept this compromise. American Jews, together with many of their counterparts in Western Europe, are caught in a quandary. The Israeli government wishes Jewish communities throughout the world to support its positions, and many of the leaders of American Jewish organizations feel that it is their responsibility to do so. They point out that it is the Israelis, not Americans or others, who are on the firing line and best know the needs of their own security. Others, however—Israelis and Americans, leaders as well as ordinary Jews—can see nothing but turmoil and warfare in the future if Israel does not come to some sort of terms with the Arab population in the occupied territories. Within the American religious organizations, many non-Orthodox leaders (Reform, Conservative, and Reconstructionist) are aligned with the Israeli "peace" camp, while a number of the Orthodox leaders support the more intransigent stand of the Israeli government. Several American Jews, as well as Israelis active in the peace movement, have been engaged in dialog with PLO representatives since 1988. Those who oppose such dialog consider this "treason to the cause of Israel."

There is another area in which tension exists between American Jews and elements in Israel. Over the years Israeli Orthodox Judaism has grown much more militant than it was in the past. Periodically, Orthodox representatives in the Israeli parliament introduce legislation to amend the

"Law of Return" so as to invalidate non-Orthodox conversions to Judaism. (The Law of Return provides that any Jew who wishes to settle in Israel is entitled to automatic citizenship once he or she arrives in the land. A Jew is defined as one who was born to a Jewish mother or who was converted to Judaism. According to its present wording, any kind of conversion is acceptable; but the Orthodox wish to amend the law to make it refer to "conversion according to halaka," which they contend means under Orthodox auspices only.) The Orthodox parties in 1988 offered to support other parties in forming a coalition government if they would, in turn, support the Orthodox amendment. They were not successful in this effort, but before the matter was decided thousands of telephone calls, telegrams, and letters from the United States reached Israeli officials, and many American Jewish leaders came to Israel in person, warning against the adoption of the amendment. As time goes on, it appears as if the outlook of American jews will continue to diverge from that of many Israelis in matters concerning the role of religion as well as in the search for peace.

Differences between American Jews and Israel are painful for those Americans who have been involved over the years with the stirring events leading to the birth of the Jewish state and its subsequent development. It would seem, however, that the future relationship between the two communities will assume a more mature form. Orthodox Jews in America emphasize more and more the obligation of religious observance as the essential element defining Jewish identity; for many this is contradictory to a sense of special relationship with a state, even the State of Israel (assuming that the state does not become Orthodox). Non-Orthodox Jews in America are coming more and more to regard their Jewishness as basically an ethnic identity, akin to being Italian-American, Chinese-American, and so on. It seems likely that, just as these Americans do not ordinarily cultivate a sense of special relationship with the state from which their ancestors came, American Jews will come to relate to the State of Israel in a similar manner. It will be the culture of Judaism, including the religious form in which it is so often manifested, rather than a political state to which American Jews will feel a bond.

CHAPTER EIGHT

The Jewish Household

The very house in which a Jew dwells is supposed to be marked on its doorpost—that is, the one on the right-hand side as one enters—with the *mezuza*, a small receptacle of metal or wood that contains two biblical passages (Deuteronomy 6:4–9 and 11:13–21) written by hand, in Hebrew, on a small piece of parchment. These are two sections of the *shema* (see p. 74). The *mezuza* serves as a reminder of God's presence and protection. Orthodox Jews affix a *mezuza* at the entrance to every room in the house except bathrooms. Non-Orthodox Jews usually are content with a *mezuza* at the main entrance to the house.

Daily Prayer

Upon awakening in the morning an observant Jew says, "I thank You, living and enduring King, that You have returned my soul to me in mercy, for great is your faithfulness." He then washes his hands. Halaka requires that a Jew wash his hands, reciting the appropriate blessing, upon rising in the morning, before meals, and after defecation. Before putting on his clothes he dons the *tallit katan*, the small garment with its four fringes (*sisit*) that he wears against his upper body. After dressing he is ready for morning prayer. If possible he will go to the synagogue to join with a congregation in prayer, but private worship is also acceptable. In the absence of a congregation of at least ten, however, certain portions of the service, such as the kaddish, have to be omitted.

A non-Orthodox Jew at morning prayer will probably put on a skullcap before beginning his devotion (an Orthodox Jew will not have to do so, since he put his on as soon as he got out of bed). Orthodox or not, he will then wrap himself in the *tallit* (the prayer shawl with knotted fringes at its four corners) and put on his phylacteries (*tefillin*). These are small leather boxes in which four biblical passages, written on parchment, have been inserted. The first two passages are Exodus 13:1–10 and 13:11–16, referring to the consecration of the first-born of both man and beast to God, the Passover, and the Exodus, which events are to be memorialized as a "sign upon your hand and as a remembrance between your eyes"; the other two passages are Deuteronomy 6:4–9 and 11:13–21, two of the sections of the *shema* that are also inserted in the *mezuza*. One phylactery is placed around the top of the head by a leather strap; the other encircles the upper left arm opposite the heart (a left-handed person wears it on his right arm). The *tefillin* are put on in obedience to God's command, "you shall bind them as a sign upon your hand and they shall be frontlets between your eyes." The worshipper is now attired in his insignia of office, as it were, for the Jew is the attendant or courtier of the Divine King. He appears before God as the day begins in the attire of royalty, that is, the *tallit* and *tefillin*. *Tefillin*, however, are not worn on the Sabbath or on holy days, since the innate sanctity of those days renders them unnecessary.

The worshipper then recites the prayers of the weekday morning service from the Siddur, removing the *tefillin* and *tallit* when he has finished. Since the service includes passages from the Torah, the Prophets, the Psalms, the Mishna and Talmud (and, in some Orthodox communities, from the Zohar as well), he has fulfilled not only the commandment of worship but also that of studying these sacred texts. A serious Jew will attempt to study every day, but if his work or other responsibilities prevent him from doing so, he has fulfilled his minimal responsibility in this regard by reciting the morning service.

After prayer, the worshipper is now eligible to eat breakfast. It should be noted that in some Hasidic groups men do not put on a *tallit* until after they are married. In Orthodoxy as a whole, women are not obligated to recite the daily prayers because of their responsibilities as keepers of the home, although they are permitted to recite them if they wish to do so.

Reform Jews do not wear a *tallit katan* and most of them do not put on *tallit* and *tefillin* when praying. Formal prayer on weekdays, in fact, is rather rare for Reform Jews and some other non-Orthodox Jews. The emphasis in these groups is on Sabbath and holy day worship. Of course, many Orthodox men do not recite the prayers daily; it is assumed that within the Orthodox community those who omit worship feel a sense of sin for not having lived up to their obligation. Reform Jews, on the other hand, do not feel that they have sinned when they fail to recite the statutory prayers. Among Conservative Jews, some feel that they should pray daily, while others feel no great concern to do so.

At mealtimes the observant Jew recites the blessing for bread, if bread is part of the meal, before he eats: "Blessed are You, Lord our God, King of the world, who brings forth bread from the earth." The major prayer of thanksgiving, however, is at the end of the meal, when he has eaten and is satisfied:

> Blessed are You, Lord our God, King of the world, who sustains the entire world through his goodness, with grace, kindness and mercy. He gives bread to all flesh, for his kindness is forever; and through his great goodness we have never lacked, nor will we have any lack of sustenance in the future. For the sake of his great name, for

He is a God who feeds and sustains all, He does good to all and prepares sustenance for all the creatures He has made. Blessed are You, Lord, who sustains all.

This grace after the meal continues for several more paragraphs. If more than three have eaten together, it is recited as a communal prayer.

The afternoon and evening services are much shorter than the morning one. In most synagogues they are recited in quick succession, near the time of sunset. The observant Jew may seek out a congregation for these services, or, as in the morning, he may recite them privately. Neither *tallit nor tefillin* are worn at these services, although often the prayer leader in a synagogue will don a *tallit*. Before retiring to bed at night it is customary to recite the *shema*.

A truly dedicated Orthodox Jew goes through life hoping that he might have the opportunity of blessing God at least a hundred times a day for the benefits that He provides. Many blessings are included in the worship services and in the grace after meals. Other blessings that a Jew might seek to recite include the benediction for new experiences ("Blessed are You, Lord our God, King of the world, for You have kept us in life, and sustained us, and brought us to this time"), that for wine ("Blessed are You, Lord our God, King of the world, creator of the fruit of the vine"), the blessing for washing the hands, and the one for emerging unscathed from danger. There are also special benedictions for eating various foods (for example, one for fruits, one for vegetables, one for grain products) and for smelling the fragrance of fruits, spices, or perfumes. There are blessings for seeing a rainbow or lightning or other impressive phenomena of nature. There is a blessing upon encountering a great scholar ("Blessed are You, Lord our God, King of the world, who has given of his wisdom to flesh and blood") and for seeing a king ("Blessed are You, Lord our God, King of the World, who has given of his glory to flesh and blood"). There is even a blessing for seeing a beautiful woman ("Blessed are You, Lord our God, King of the world, who has created such in his world"). The Talmud tells of a great sage who recited this benediction upon seeing a particularly beautiful woman. His contemporaries wondered how this could be, since pious Jews, particularly rabbinical scholars, are not supposed to look at an unknown woman. They concluded, according to the Talmud, that he accidentally saw the woman while turning a corner.

The Sabbath

Whether Orthodox, Reform, Conservative, or Reconstructionist, for Jews who take their religion seriously, the Sabbath is the most significant day of the week. In fact, the Sabbath is the most important day in one's life, for it is on that day that heaven and earth meet. It is the time when the Jew can have a foretaste of the world-to-come. Harsh judgment is assuaged, and God and the Jewish people come together in loving embrace. The mystics portrayed the Sabbath as the Queen, the Shekina or Bride of God who comes to Him and to his people every Friday at sunset and remains until the following sunset. The symbolism of the mystics has infused the poetry of all the forms of Judaism. Consider the hymn with which the Sabbath is greeted on Friday night:

Come, beloved, to greet the Bride; let us bid welcome to the Sabbath. . . . Come in peace, O Crown of your Husband, come with joy and song to the faithful of your treasured people. Come, Bride, come, Sabbath Queen.

On Saturday night the Hasidim and other groups of Jews celebrate the "escort of the Queen" as she leaves her people at the start of the workweek. There is a touch of sadness as the Sabbath departs, but there is also the anticipatory joy of her return and the blessings that she will bring.

For this reason Jews who observe the Sabbath by abstaining from the activities forbidden on that day do not feel any sense of deprivation. On the contrary, they maintain that those who do not abstain from these activities are the ones who are deprived, because they are unable to partake of the extra measure of holiness that is inherent in the day. Jews who do not drive their automobiles or turn on electrical appliances on the Sabbath (unless they are obeying these rules strictly out of habit, without knowledge or appreciation of the day's significance) are not envious of their neighbors who do these things, for they believe that the joy inherent in the day more than makes up for what they have given up. Workday activities are set aside not merely because the law must be obeyed, but in order to make room for the study, the song, the prayer, and the joyous feasting that makes the day so special.

In a traditional Jewish household the husband attends the Sabbath evening service in the synagogue while the wife remains at home to prepare the meal and set the table. Before sunset she lights and blesses the Sabbath candles: "Blessed are You, Lord our God, King of the world, for You have sanctified us by your commandments and commanded us to kindle the Sabbath light." When the husband returns from the synagogue he might chant the hymn *shalom aleikem*, welcoming the angels who come to grace the household on the Sabbath. He might then bless his wife with the words from Proverbs 31, beginning "a woman of valor who can find, for her price is far above rubies." He would then bless his children; for girls he would use the words "the Lord make you like Sarah, Rebecca, Rachel, and Leah"; for boys he would say, "the Lord make you like Ephraim and Manasseh." Then he blesses the entire family. "The Lord bless you and keep you. The Lord cause his countenance to shine upon you and be gracious unto you. The Lord lift up his countenance toward you and grant you peace." In Hasidic homes, or in other families where the mystical tradition is cherished, the hymn *atkinu seudata* is chanted. This celebrates the marriage of God and his Shekina, and begins,

We have prepared the banquet of Faith, the perfect wedding feast for the Holy King. We have prepared the banquet for the King, this being the banquet to honor the Field of Holy Apple Trees [an epithet of the Shekina]. And the Small Countenance [an epithet of the Holy King] and the Holy Ancient One come to banquet with Her.

Before the meal begins the husband chants the *kiddush*, the sanctification of the wine and the day:

Blessed are You, Lord our God, King of the world, creator of the fruit of the vine. Blessed are You, Lord our God, King of the world, who has sanctified us by his commandments and taken pleasure in us, and has caused us to inherit his holy Sabbath in love and in favor, a memorial of the act of Creation. For it is the first of the holy days, a remembrance of the Exodus from Egypt. For You have chosen us, and sanctified us from among all peoples, and your holy Sabbath in love and in favor have You given us as an inheritance. Blessed are You, Lord, who sanctifies the Sabbath.

The family then shares the wine. The husband breaks bread and blesses it: "Blessed are You, Lord our God, King of the world, who brings forth bread from the earth." The Sabbath bread, a special braided loaf called *halla*, is then distributed.

The Sabbath evening meal is supposed to be the best of the week, and even the poor who cannot afford luxuries during the week make an effort to eat well at this time. There is often both a fish course and a meat course. After the meal is finished a number of Sabbath songs might be sung. These are Hebrew and Aramaic hymns that celebrate the joys of the sacred day, as well as God's love for Israel and the blessings that will come when Israel and the world will be redeemed. The celebration concludes with the chanting of the grace after the meal.

In observant but non-Orthodox families the wife and children often share in leading the various blessings at the table with the husband. In many non-Orthodox households this relaxed type of Sabbath evening meal might not take place because the synagogue that the family attends holds a "late Friday night" service. This practice originated in Reform Judaism. Instead of scheduling Sabbath evening worship at sunset, congregations that follow this pattern schedule the service after the dinner hour so that entire families can attend together. After a service of this type, which would usually include a sermon or lecture, there would likely be a social hour with refreshments for all who attended.

In most synagogues, other than many Reform ones, the major service of the week takes place on Saturday morning. Although Orthodox women are not obligated according to halaka to attend, many of them do (though, of course, they do not sit with the men). Men, except many in Reform synagogues, wear the *tallit* at this service. When the family returns home after the service, they sit down to another hearty meal. In observant families, no new food may be cooked on the Sabbath, but if the stove or oven was put on before the Sabbath began, food may be warmed over a low flame, and when the time comes for the Sabbath noon meal to be served, it is often very delicious. During Sabbath afternoons, friends may be visited (provided that they live within walking distance), but the truly devoted would always set aside part of the day for religious study. It is customary for the "third meal" to be served before sunset on Saturday, while it is still Sabbath, so as to enhance the pleasure of the day. Sometimes synagogues sponsor a "third meal" at which a lecture is presented and Sabbath songs are sung. Following the afternoon service in the synagogue, as well as the evening service to inaugurate the new day that begins at sunset, the *habdala* is recited. (At home it may be recited anytime after sunset). This involves the kindling and blessing of a braided candle and the blessing of some aromatic spices and a cup of wine, after which the following is chanted:

Blessed are You, Lord our God, King of the world, who separates between the sacred and the profane, between light and darkness, between Israel and the peoples, between the seventh day and the six days of labor. Blessed are You, Lord, who separates the sacred from the profane.

The wine is then drunk and the candle extinguished. The spices are part of the ceremony in order to revive the soul of the Jew, for it is saddened by the departure of the Sabbath Queen.

The Dietary Rules

One of the ways in which a Jewish household maintains a tie to the generations of the past—and to Jews living in all parts of the world—is through its observance of the dietary restrictions. Reform Judaism allows the abrogation of these rules, although a number of Reform Jews choose to keep some of them. The other branches of Judaism emphasize the importance of the dietary laws, although truly Orthodox Jews, of course, observe them with greater rigor and attention to detail. (Some Jews who like to attend Orthodox or Conservative synagogues nonetheless disregard all of the dietary laws. Technically they are sinners, at least in this one area of practice, in the eyes of the branch of Judaism that they have chosen for themselves.)

The dietary restrictions are contained in the rules of *kashrut* ("fitness"), specifying which animals are *kosher*, or fit for Jewish consumption. Only animals that have a split hoof and chew a cud are acceptable; other animals, such as the pig (which has a split hoof but does not chew the cud), are forbidden. Another rule of *kashrut* is that a kosher animal must be slaughtered properly, in accordance with ancient ritual practice, in order for Jews to eat its meat. The ritual slaughterer, or *shohet,* is trained in the procedure, which basically requires one swift incision in the jugular vein so that blood gushes out in large volume and the animal is rendered unconscious almost instantaneously. The *shohet* also examines the inner organs of slaughtered animals, particularly the lungs, to see if there is any evidence of disease that would render the meat unfit for consumption. According to the rules of *kashrut*, as much blood as possible must be withdrawn from the meat before it can be eaten, since "the blood is the life," and this must return to God rather than be consumed by human beings. For this reason kosher meat must be salted with a coarse type of salt, either by the butcher in his shop or by the purchaser at home, and then thoroughly washed before it is cooked. The salting and washing help remove much of the blood that may have remained in the meat. (Meat roasted over an open flame does not require salting.)

Sea creatures must have both fins and scales in order to be kosher. This leaves out all shellfish. There are no particular procedures for preparing fish that are specified by the rules of *kashrut*, but there are disputes between various authorities from time to time as to whether particular species of fish are kosher, because some fish have scales in early development but lose them as they mature. Some consider swordfish and certain varieties of sturgeon to be kosher, while others do not. This is an important question for those who want to know if they are allowed to eat caviar.

Besides specifying the types of animals that Jews may eat, and the proper procedures for slaughtering them, the laws of *kashrut* prohibit the mixing of any milk product with any meat product at the same meal. This derives from the biblical law, "You shall not cook the young in its mother's milk." The early rabbis extended this biblical prohibition to include the consumption of any item made from milk together with any item containing meat or animal fat. The halaka eventually came to include even fowl as a "meat" that could not be eaten together with milk, though this was not the case originally. The rabbis then made another "fence" around the law by requiring that separate utensils, dishes, and pots be kept for milk foods and meat foods. Orthodox Jews also use kosher soap and separate towels for drying milk and meat dishes. After eating a milk food, the rule is that one must wait a short while before eating a meat food. After eating meat, one must wait three to six hours before eating a milk food, to insure that digestion is complete.*

Though some people maintain that hygienic factors underlie the dietary laws, in actuality they serve to consecrate the Jew to the service of God. Religious Jews take pride in the special discipline that requires them to keep the different foods separate and in the knowledge that there are foods that all other peoples in the world may eat except Jews, who are God's "special people." Wealthy Orthodox families may have separate stoves and ovens and sinks for meat and milk foods, or separate refrigerators, or, in an example of extreme devotion to the law, separate kitchens.

The Birth of a Child

When a boy is born to a Jewish family, the rite of circumcision, called the covenant of circumcision (*brit mila*), is supposed to take place when the child is eight days old. The only Jewish males exempt from this obligation are those whose life or health would be endangered by the operation, such as hemophiliacs. The operation must be performed on the eighth day of life even if that day happens to be the Sabbath, the Day of Atonement, or another Jewish holiday. The only acceptable reason for postponing the procedure is medical necessity: If a physician states that the operation should be delayed, then his instructions are followed. Ritual circumcisions are ordinarily performed by a specially trained expert, a *mohel*. A minyan of ten should be present at a circumcision, or if that is not possible, at least three Jewish men.

*Observant Jews never eat meat from the hind quarters of cattle or sheep. This prohibition derives from Genesis 32:32, which relates that when Jacob wrestled with the mysterious being who bestowed upon him the name "Israel," he was injured in the "sinew of the hip that is on the hollow of the thigh." Kosher butchers ordinarily turn over the hind quarters of animals they have slaughtered (which include sirloin steak and filet mignon cuts) to purveyors of non-kosher meat.

The major part of the ritual, chanted by the *mohel* over a cup of wine after the actual operation has been performed, is as follows:

> Blessed are You, Lord our God, King of the world, creator of the fruit of the vine. Blessed are You, Lord our God, King of the world, who has sanctified the beloved from the womb and set your statute in his flesh, and sealed his offspring with the sign of the holy covenant. Therefore because of this, living God, our portion and our rock, deliver the dearly beloved of our flesh for the sake of the covenant You have set within us. Blessed are You, Lord, who makes the covenant.
>
> Our God and God of our fathers, preserve this child to his father and his mother and let his name be called in Israel [the name of the infant is given]. Let his father rejoice in his offspring and let his mother be glad in the fruit of her womb. As it is written, "Let your father and mother rejoice, and let her that bore you be glad." And it is said, "I passed by you and saw you weltering in your blood and I said to you, In your blood you shall live, yea in your blood you shall live." And it is said, "He has remembered his covenant forever, the word which He commanded to a thousand generations, that which He established with Abraham and his oath unto Isaac and set unto Jacob as a statute, to Israel as an everlasting covenant." And it is said, "Abraham circumcised his son Isaac when he was eight days old, as God had commanded him." Give thanks unto the Lord, for He is good; his mercy endures forever. This little child, may he become great. And as he has entered into the covenant, so may he enter into the study of the Torah, into marriage, and into a lifetime of good deeds.

During this prayer, the infant is usually given a drop of wine, both to enable him to participate in the celebration and to quiet him down after the procedure. At its conclusion all present partake of a festive repast. Orthodox and

Conservative and many Reform Jews call upon a *mohel* for this traditional ritual. Some Reform Jews, however, have a physician perform the circumcision in the hospital as a purely medical procedure a day or two after the child is born, and then ask their congregational rabbi to name and bless the child either at a synagogue service or at a celebration at home on the eighth day.

When a girl is born to a Jewish family, no medical procedure analogous to the circumcision takes place. Among Orthodox Jews the father will attend a synagogue service on a Sabbath morning or on a Monday or Thursday morning when the Torah is read sometime after the child's birth and arrange to be one of those called up for blessing during the reading of the Torah. During the blessing, God's favor will be invoked upon the child and a Hebrew name bestowed. In many Conservative congregations both the father and the mother will go up during the reading of the Torah for this procedure. Among Reform Jews, the usual practice used to be for the child to be named during a synagogue service, but in recent years many Reform Jews, as well as Conservative and Reconstructionist Jews, have taken to arranging home ceremonies and celebrations to commemorate the birth of a girl, on the order of what is done for a boy. The wording of the ritual might be an adaptation of the words used at a circumcision, or it could be an original composition by the attending rabbi or the parents or be derived from some other source. A ceremony of this type for a girl is often called *brit hayyim* ("covenant of life").

There is no single tradition that governs all Jews with regard to the choice of a child's name. Many Jews whose ancestry stems from Eastern Europe have the custom of always naming a child after a deceased relative. Sephardic Jews, on the other hand, have the custom of naming a child after grandparents, whether living or dead. Most Jewish children are given both a Hebrew name and a secular one. Many families strive to choose names in which there is a noticeable relationship between the Hebrew and secular names, such as similarity in meaning or in sound; other families, however, are not concerned with this.

In observant Jewish families there is an additional ceremony when a first-born son is thirty days old. This is the *pidyon haben* ("redemption of the first-born"), deriving from Exodus 13:12–13: "You shall set apart to the Lord all that first opens the womb. All the firstlings of your cattle that are males shall be the Lord's. . . . Every first-born of man among your sons you shall redeem." In this procedure a *kohen* (a descendant of the priestly line of Aaron) is given a sum of money as a redemption for the child. The *kohen* subsequently gives the money to charity. If the father is himself a *kohen* or a Levite, or if the mother is the daughter of a *kohen* or a Levite, this ritual is not performed.

Coming of Age

When a Jewish boy reaches his thirteenth birthday he automatically becomes a *bar mitsva* ("son of the commandments"); that is, he is religiously an adult, qualified to be counted as a member of a minyan, the quorum for worship, and qualified to serve as a leader in worship if he is sufficiently knowledgeable to be able to do so. He is obligated to observe the ethical and ritual teachings of the religion, the commandments both negative and positive. No ceremony is necessary for him to assume this new status. Over the centuries, however, it became customary for families to celebrate a son's becoming a *bar mitsva* by having him participate in a synagogue ceremony near the time of his thirteenth birthday, and for relatives and friends to enjoy a festive repast thereafter. In common parlance the ceremony in the synagogue and the attendant party is called a "Bar Mitsva."

Bar Mitsva ceremonies may take place in a synagogue at any time when the Torah is read, most often at a Sabbath morning service. Many synagogues require that young people complete a certain number of years of religious school study before they are allowed to have the ceremony. These studies include Hebrew and Jewish history and theology. At the ceremony the young man is for the first time called up to the public reading of the Torah. He chants the benedictions before and after the reading of the biblical lesson and a few verses from the Torah scroll itself. He then chants the benedictions that accompany the reading of the lesson from the Prophets (the *haftara*), as well as the lesson itself. There is often a short speech about the significance of the occasion by the boy, followed by a blessing of the boy by the rabbi.

Until the 1920s there was no ceremony to mark the coming of age of a girl. Over the years, however, Conservative, Reform, and Reconstructionist congregations developed the *Bat Mitsva* ("daughter of the commandments") ceremony. In congregations attached to these movements, girls participate in the ritual in the same manner as Bar Mitsva boys when they are of age and have completed the requisite studies. In Orthodox synagogues, on the other hand, since women are not permitted to read from the Torah scroll before a congregation, the Bat Mitsva ceremony either does not exist or it takes an alternative form, such as allowing the girl to read other selections or give a talk on a religious theme.

During its early years in Germany and the United States, Reform Judaism developed the ceremony of Confirmation as a replacement for the traditional Bar Mitsva. Confirmation is a group exercise, tantamount to graduation from a synagogue's religious school, rather than a ceremony centered about an individual. In most cases it involves a statement of faith or commitment on the part of those being "confirmed" in the religious tradition. Many Reform temples provide Bar and Bat Mitsva at age thirteen and Confirmation at age fifteen or sixteen. In most communities today, relatively few young people avail themselves of the opportunity to continue their studies until Confirmation. It is the Bar Mitsva that has remained paramount as the Jewish coming-of-age ceremony, hallowed as it is by the practice of centuries past.

Marriage and Family Purity

The Jewish marriage ceremony is preceded by the signing of the *ketuba*, the marriage contract, (originally designed for the economic protection of the woman), by the two official witnesses to the ceremony that will take place. In Orthodox practice these witnesses must be two Jewish men who are unrelated by blood to either the bride or the groom and unrelated to each other. Many Orthodox rabbis require that the witnesses be strict Sabbath observers. The non-Orthodox forms of Judaism have no objection to the use of women as official witnesses.

After the signing of the *ketuba*, the wedding party moves into the room where the *huppa* is set up, the groom escorted by his parents and the bride by her parents. (The *huppa* is a canopy under which the bride and groom stand during the ceremony. It may be attached to poles that are held by four people or it may be part of a stationary structure that is perhaps elaborately decorated with flowers.) The rabbi or cantor or other person officiating begins with an invocation and then often addresses some personal words to the bride and groom. This is followed by the blessing of the first cup of wine, representing betrothal or the intention to marry, which is then sipped by the bride and groom. In non-Orthodox ceremonies this is followed by an exchange of vows between bride and groom; Orthodox ceremonies would not necessarily include this since it is not part of ancient Jewish practice.

The groom next places a ring on the bride's finger, repeating these words: "Be consecrated (meaning "set aside") unto me by this ring according to the law of Moses and Israel." In non-Orthodox ceremonies the bride will often place a ring on the groom's finger, but this is not done in Orthodoxy, since such a custom is a completely modern innovation with no basis in traditional Judaism. After the giving of the ring the *ketuba* is read, though this is often omitted in Reform Judaism. Next come the "seven benedictions" chanted over the second cup of wine, that representing marriage. Included in them are these words:

> May You gladden the beloved as You did gladden your creation in the Garden of Eden in days of yore. Blessed are You, Lord, who gladdens the bridegroom and the bride. Blessed are You, Lord our God, King of the world, who has created joy and gladness, bridegroom and bride, rejoicing, song, pleasure and delight, love and brotherhood, peace and fellowship. Soon, Lord our God, may there be heard in the cities of Judah and the streets of Jerusalem the voice of joy and gladness, the voice of the bridegroom and the voice of the bride, the jubilant voice of bridegrooms from their nuptial canopies and of youths from their feasts of song. Blessed are You, Lord, who gladdens the bridegroom together with the bride.

After the bride and groom drink from the cup the groom shatters a glass (a well-wrapped one, stamping upon it with the heel of his shoe). The traditional explanation for this custom is that it is a remembrance of the destruction of the Temple of Jerusalem. In actuality it stems from the Middle Ages, originating as a gesture to insure good fortune (*mazzal tob*) and drive away any evil spirits who might be lurking in the vicinity of the wedding celebration. A similar act is recounted in Talmud Berakot 31a.

In Orthodox and Conservative practice, the bride and groom are taken to a room where they are left alone for a short while immediately after the wedding ceremony. This is symbolic of their first marital intercourse, since no marriage is valid unless it is consummated by intercourse.

Judaism is insistent that sexual relations may take place only between a man and a woman who are married to each other. This does not mean, however, that a child who is born out of wedlock is illegitimate. A child born to an unmarried Jewish woman is a fully legitimate Jew, subject to no religious disability whatever. The halakic category of bastard (*mamzer*) is applicable only to a child born of incest or adultery, with adultery defined as intercourse with a woman who is married or betrothed to another man. A *mamzer*, according to halaka, is unable to marry a legitimate Jew. A married man who has intercourse with an unattached woman is condemned by Jewish law and tradition, but is not guilty of adultery. He is guilty, rather, of lewd behavior, such as no self-respecting Jew should want to commit. He is, fortunately, not subject to the death penalty which, according to biblical law, could theoretically be exacted of both the man and the woman in a case of true adultery attested by at least two acceptable witnesses.

Orthodox Judaism is very concerned to encourage the practice of "family purity." This is based upon the commandment in Leviticus 15 that a woman is forbidden sexually to her husband during her menstrual period. The rabbis legislated that a woman must wait seven days after her menstrual flow has ceased. She must then go to a *mikveh*, a ritual bath built in accordance with halakic specifications, and immerse herself in its waters before she and her husband may come together again. Many Orthodox women of child-bearing age look forward each month to their visit to the *mikveh*. They not only anticipate the sexual union that they will enjoy thereafter, but they are conscious of their role as mothers of the "holy people," a role that becomes dramatically evident in their visits to the *mikveh* and the practice of "family purity." The Talmud comments,

> Why did the Torah ordain that the (ritual) uncleanness of menstruation should continue for seven days? Because after being in constant contact with his wife a husband might find her repulsive. The Torah therefore ordained: Let her be unclean for these days in order that she shall be beloved by her husband as at the time of her first entry into the bridal chamber. (Nidda 31b).

Reform Jewish women, other than an exceptional few, do not go to the *mikveh*. Some Conservative women do, but most do not. (Practically every *mikveh* is closed to women on

Fridays, since that is when Hasidic and other very Orthodox men go to purify themselves for the Sabbath.)

With regard to birth control, most Jewish families utilize various forms, though Orthodox Judaism encourages its people to fulfill the commandment to "be fruitful and multiply." Within Orthodoxy it is only the woman who is permitted to take measures that will prevent conception; the man is prohibited from doing so. Abortion is not equated with murder, though it is condemned by Orthodoxy except in cases where it is necessary for the life or health of the mother. (Under rabbinic law a fetus is not thought of as a "soul" until it is born; prior to that time it is a "limb of its mother.")

Jewish law permits divorce, though historically most Jewish communities have evidenced low divorce rates. A Jewish document of divorce, called a *get*, must be commissioned by the husband and written by a trained scribe. It must then be placed in the hands of the wife in the presence of witnesses. There is no corresponding procedure by which a wife can present her husband with a divorce. Reform Judaism has eliminated the need for religious divorce and accepts the decree of a civil court as sufficient to terminate a marriage. Orthodox and Conservative Judaism, however, still insist that the Jewish divorce procedure be followed after a civil divorce has been obtained. If this is not done, a woman who remarries is guilty of adultery in the judgment of these groups. Children born of this second union are theoretically illegitimate, except in the eyes of Reform Judaism. Such children, according to halaka, are ineligible to marry Jews of untainted ancestry.

Conversion to Judaism

All the branches of Judaism would agree that if a person who is not Jewish should come to believe that much of the theology with which he or she was raised is mistaken, that God has indeed chosen the Jews as his "special people" and given them his unique law as contained in both the written Scriptures and the teachings of the rabbis, to be adhered to for all time, then that person should seriously consider conversion to Judaism. For Orthodoxy this is the only acceptable reason for conversion to Judaism. Reform and Reconstructionist Judaism, however, also look upon marriage to a Jew as an eminently desirable motive for conversion, contributing to a unified family and providing a harmonious atmosphere in which to bring up Jewish children. These groups also welcome converts who may have grown up without any real religious heritage of their own, but who subsequently find themselves attracted to Jewish teachings and the Jewish way of life. Within Conservative Judaism there is a difference of opinion. Most Conservative rabbis are probably close to the Reform position, but many lean toward the Orthodox attitude.

Instruction leading to conversion includes courses in Jewish history and theology, the Bible and rabbinic texts, the observance of the Sabbath and holidays, the making of a Jewish home, the prayers in the synagogue, and the rudiments of reading Hebrew. Candidates are taught that the first step in becoming a Jew is the acceptance of "the yoke of the kingdom of Heaven"—that is, the sovereignty of the One God over all that is or will be. The second step is the acceptance of "the yoke of the commandments." According to Orthodox Judaism, the commandments are embodied in the halaka, both the ethical and ritual requirements spelled out in the Scriptures, the Talmud, and the later codes of law. Orthodox rabbis generally will not accept the validity of non-Orthodox conversions because, they say, the convert who is instructed by a Conservative, Reform, or Reconstructionist rabbi is not taught that he or she must live by halaka. Learning Jewish history and philosophy is not enough; there must be an indoctrination in how to live according to Jewish ritual law, including the dietary restrictions and the rules of "family purity." Since the other branches of Judaism do not sufficiently emphasize these matters, Orthodox Judaism does not accept their conversions. The other

branches, however, accept the validity of Orthodox conversions. Among Conservative rabbis there is a variation in
practice. Some accept the validity of Reform conversions,
particularly if the halakic rituals that symbolize conversion
have been utilized, while others do not.

Courses of instruction for conversion may last from three
months to a year. If at the conclusion of the course the
candidate still wishes to become a Jew and is willing to
foreswear allegiance to any other religion, the rabbi will
make arrangements for the ritual ceremonies that induct
one into Judaism. In many cases the rabbi calls on two
rabbinic colleagues so that the three together can constitute
a "rabbinic court" to examine the candidate about his or her
knowledge of Judaism. The next step would be, in the case
of a male convert, the ritual circumcision performed by a
mohel. In the case of someone who had already been medi-
cally circumcised, the *mohel* draws a symbolic "drop of
blood of the covenant" in order to satisfy the ritual requirement. (Circumcision, of course, is dispensed with if a physician certifies that it would be dangerous for the convert to
undergo it.) The final step, in the case of both men and
women, is immersion in the ritual bath (*mikveh*). The rabbi
arranges for the court of three rabbis, or perhaps the rabbi
and two laymen, to witness the immersion of the unclothed
convert in the pool of water. In the case of a woman, the
group of men stay outside the door for reasons of modesty
and depend on the word of a female witness that the convert
had immersed herself fully in the *mikveh.* If the convert is a
man and the rabbi or a witness is a woman, which could
occur in the non-Orthodox branches of Judaism, a similar
procedure would be followed. The convert emerges from
the water as a new person, bearing a Hebrew name and
reborn as the youngest child of Abraham and Sarah.

The ritual in Reform Judaism is often different from what
has been described. Reform does not require adult circumcision, nor does it require immersion in the *mikveh.* Many
Reform conversions do not include these rites, though a
number of converts elect to have one or both of them. In

the majority of cases the rabbi conducts a conversion ceremony at the synagogue or at home, blessing and welcoming
the convert into the fellowship of the Jewish faith and people in the presence of an assembly of family and friends.

A convert is a full Jew in every respect. Halaka forbids a
Jew from embarrassing a convert by referring to his or her
former status. Though a female convert may not marry a
kohen, her children are allowed to do so. (Reform Judaism
does not prohibit the marriage of a *kohen* to a convert.)

Death

If a Jew knows that he is near death he should recite,
"Hear, Israel, the Lord is our God, the Lord is One," and if
possible confess his sins. It is not necessary for anyone to be
present to hear this, since it is directed only to God. After
death the body is generally released to a mortuary and the
funeral is scheduled, if possible, for the day following death.
Embalming is not permitted by Orthodoxy unless the burial
must be delayed. Some very Orthodox groups bury their
dead on the day of death if it occurred sufficiently early in
the morning for arrangements to be made. An acceptable
reason to delay a burial is to await the arrival of family
members who must travel a long distance. Since funerals
and burials are not allowed on the Sabbath or major Jewish
holidays, a number will be delayed for this reason as well.

In general, funeral services are held at synagogues only
for people who have been active in the work of the congregation. Most often funerals are held at a funeral home or,
occasionally, at the home of the deceased. The casket should
be a simple one made of wood. The body should be dressed
in a simple white shroud, since all are equal in death, and a
man is buried with his *tallit*. (Reform Jews, however, are
often buried in their usual clothes.) In many Orthodox
communities a volunteer group known as the *hevra kaddisha*
("holy brotherhood") washes and dresses the body. Except
in the case of some Reform families, flowers should not be

sent to Jewish funerals. Charitable contributions in memory of the deceased are the preferred form of tribute. Gifts of food to the bereaved family are acceptable.

Jewish law is specific about which relatives are obligated to mourn a death in a ritual way. These would include the sons, daughters, father, mother, husband or wife, brothers and sisters. In Orthodox families these mourners rend their garment when a death occurs or when they first learn of it. They say, "Blessed is the righteous Judge." Among non-Orthodox Jews the rending of garments is rare. Instead, just before the beginning of the funeral service the funeral director pins a black ribbon on the mourner's blouse or jacket and then cuts the ribbon. This ribbon is worn by the mourners for thirty days, except on the Sabbath. At the funeral service itself psalms and prayers are recited, but the heart of the service is usually the eulogy of the deceased. Not only the person officiating, but also friends and relatives are often encouraged to speak about the deceased and the spiritual legacy that he or she leaves behind.

Even though traditional Judaism believes in the eternal life of the soul and the resurrection of the dead, these themes are rarely alluded to in the remarks made at funerals, even among the Orthodox. The memorial prayer recited just before the remains are to be carried to the grave site is the following:

> God full of compassion, who dwells on high, grant perfect rest under the wings of the Shekina, among the holy and pure who shine as the brightness of the firmament, to the soul of [the name of the deceased is given] who has gone unto eternity. May the Lord of mercy shelter (him) (her) forever under the cover of his wings, and may (his) (her) soul be bound in the bond of eternal life. The Lord be (his) (her) possession, and may his repose be peace, and we say Amen.

Burial is the only way for a body to be disposed of in traditional Judaism, although cremation is acceptable for

Reform Jews. The interment service at the cemetery is very short, although in Orthodoxy it cannot be completed until after the casket has been lowered and the grave completely filled. The burial concludes with the recital of the kaddish by the mourners.

After burial the mourners return home to the "meal of recovery," usually bread and hard-boiled eggs, and they kindle a candle that is to burn for seven days. These are the days of *shiva* ("seven"), during which friends and family visit to console them. In more traditional families, worship services with a minyan are held morning and evening in the house of mourning for seven days (except on the Sabbath, when formal mourning is suspended). Also in traditional households the mirrors are covered since they represent vanity; the mourners do not wear leather shoes, nor do they sit on couches or soft chairs or chairs with a back when visitors are present. At the end of the seven days, which some families reduce to three if circumstances prevent their staying away from work for all seven, the mourners resume their normal way of life but abstain from going to parties or amusements for the remainder of the thirty-day period while they continue to wear the torn garment or ribbon. Mourners are expected to attend synagogue services morning and evening during the remainder of the thirty days and participate in the recitation of the "mourner's kaddish." In Orthodoxy this duty is incumbent only upon men. Mourners who go to synagogues that do not offer daily worship services have to be content with attending only on the Sabbaths. Orthodox Jews also abstain from listening to music, other than the chants in the synagogue, during the thirty days of the mourning period.

Although formal mourning is ended after thirty days, the mourners should observe each anniversary of death (*yahrzeit* in Yiddish) by lighting a candle and attending the synagogue on that day or on the nearest Sabbath and reciting the mourner's kaddish. When a parent dies, the duty of mourning and reciting the kaddish in his or her memory by the children is extended from thirty days to eleven months.

Many Jews, in all the branches of Judaism, arrange their affairs so that they can attend synagogue services once or twice a day for this eleven-month period when a parent has died. In this way they are able to publicly affirm that extra measure of gratitude and devotion that they owe to the parents who brought them into being and raised and sustained them in love.

It is the teaching of Orthodox Judaism that the souls of the righteous after death enjoy the radiance of the Divine Presence. The souls of the wicked are consigned to punishment, but, according to the tradition, only the grotesquely evil are subject to eternal damnation. The average person who may not be quite saintly enough to be worthy of the Divine Presence at the time of death needs, it is assumed, no more than one year of chastisement before he or she will be admitted to the rewards that await the righteous. It is for this reason that it became customary during the Middle Ages for sons to recite the mourner's kaddish for a year after the death of a parent. This soon became reduced to eleven months, though, since no son should want to give the impression that his parent was in need of the full year of chastisement.

Many people, both Jews and others, do not have a clear picture of what the different branches of Judaism teach about the survival of the soul after death. Orthodoxy teaches that the soul continues to exist after death and that, at the end of days, it will be restored to the body that it left behind for final judgment. Reform Judaism explicitly rejects the idea of the resurrection of the body, although for most of its existence, Reform Judaism has strongly affirmed the conviction that the human soul continues to live on in another dimension following the death of the body. In more recent times, however, a great many Reform Jews as well as some Conservative Jews have ceased to believe this, holding instead that "when you're dead, you're dead." Reconstructionists for the most part do not believe in either bodily resurrection or the survival of the soul. The fact that so many Jews do not actively believe in the survival of the soul after death has led many to state, even in print, that "Judaism" does not believe in the survival of the soul after death, and that this is one of the major differences between Judaism on the one hand and Christianity and Islam on the other. Nothing could be further from the truth. No form of Judaism has ever denied the conviction that the soul survives after death, even if a great many non-Orthodox Jews do not currently subscribe to that belief.

What might legitimately be said is that Jews in general, the Orthodox as well as the non-Orthodox, do not stress a belief in the survival of the soul as a major aspect of Jewish commitment. There are relatively few Jews of any persuasion who would say that they participate in religious life because they hope for a heavenly reward. Jews who participate in religious life do so because they are motivated by a desire to see the people and its traditions live in perpetuity, not because they are particularly concerned for the survival of their individual souls. One of the rabbinic sages of the second century B.C. described it this way: "Be not like servants who serve their Master for the sake of reward, but be like servants who serve their Master without heed to the reward (Abot 1:3)." Even if there is a heavenly reward for having lived a pious life, he taught, this should not be the reason for choosing righteousness over its opposite. Religious Jews have over the centuries tried to take these words to heart; it has been the welfare of the community in which they live, as well as the desire that the people and its ways might live on into generations yet unborn, that have motivated them to live and pray as they do, rather than a hope for heavenly reward.

CHAPTER NINE

The Calendar and Holy Days

The traditional numbering of the years in the Jewish calendar dates from the creation of the world. This was not always the case. In biblical times the years were numbered in accordance with the accession of the various kings. During the Seleucid Empire, Jews and others adopted the "Seleucid Era," which remained in use long after the empire had ceased to exist. The Romans counted their years "from the founding of Rome," and many Jews utilized that system. Over time various scholars had calculated what they believed to be the age of the world based on the ages of the patriarchs mentioned in the book of Genesis, and some Jews chose to follow that method of enumerating the years. After the Christian Church began to number the years from the birth of Jesus, Jews everywhere turned to counting the years from the creation of the world, since they felt a need to use their own religiously based system. If one wishes to translate a year "A.D." into the Jewish system, all he need do is add 3760. Thus, the major portion of 1990 is represented by the Jewish year 5750.

The Jewish cycle of months is much more ancient than the numbering of years, being derived from the calendar of Babylonia and Assyria. Each month begins with a new moon and is twenty-nine or thirty days long. Synchronizing

180

the lunar year of 354 days with the solar year of 365¼ days requires periodic leap years in which not merely an extra day but an entire additional month is added. The Jewish New Year's Day is *Rosh haShana,* coming at the new moon near the fall equinox. The following is the cycle of months from the beginning of the Jewish calendar year: *Tishri* (September–October), *Heshvan* (October–November), *Kislev* (November–December), *Tebet* (December–January), *Shebat* (January–February), *Adar* (February–March), *Nisan* (March –April), *Iyyar* (April–May), *Sivan* (May–June), *Tammuz* (June–July), *Ab* (July–August), and *Elul* (August–September).

Leap years occur in accordance with a nineteen-year cycle. A "second Adar"is added during the third, sixth, eighth, eleventh, fourteenth, seventeenth, and nineteenth years of the cycle.

Rosh haShana and Yom Kippur

Rosh haShana, the New Year, is celebrated on the first two days of Tishri, with Yom Kippur, the Day of Atonement, falling on the tenth day of the month. (Most Reform Jews observe Rosh haShana for only one day.) These holy days, like the Sabbath, are deemed to begin at sunset and conclude at sunset, as do the other holidays that occur through the year. Jews customarily speak of Rosh haShana and Yom Kippur as the "High Holy Days." These holy days open and close a ten-day period called the "Ten Days of Penitence." Work is prohibited by halaka and tradition on the holy days. On Rosh haShana certain activities may be performed that are prohibited on the Sabbath, but on Yom Kippur the prohibitions are even more stringent than on the Sabbath.

Although the High Holy Days assert the theme of penitence, one should not think of them as somber or sad. They affirm the universal sovereignty of God, and He is acclaimed as both Father and King. These holy days are, in

fact, joyous occasions, for the assurance of his pardon makes
for happiness. Rosh haShana begins with a festive meal,
including the blessing of the candles by the woman of the
house and the *kiddush* over the wine by the man, and
during the day after the service in the synagogue is over
there is a celebratory meal as well. It is customary on Rosh
haShana to eat a piece of apple or bread dipped in honey,
symbolic of the hope for a "sweet year." Yom Kippur is
preceded by a meal, though it should conclude before sundown, when the holy day begins, since the day itself is one
of fasting from both food and drink. Children and the sick
are exempt from the fast. At the conclusion of the synagogue services for the day, after sundown, families return
home to break their fast.

Rosh haShana and Yom Kippur are the days when more
Jews attend synagogue services than at any other time.
Besides the prayers that are recited every day of the year,
such as the *shema,* there are special prayers and Scripture
lessons and beautiful liturgical poetry, much of it composed
during the Middle Ages. The service on Rosh haShana
morning includes the blowing of the *shofar* (ram's horn), an
instrument used since biblical times to assemble the people
for great or sacred occasions and to awaken the impulse of
repentance. At the conclusion of the last service on Yom
Kippur the *shofar* is again sounded to signify that the fast is
over.

One of the prayers recited on both days is the following:

> Therefore, Lord our God, place your fear upon all your
> works and awe for You upon everything that You have
> created, that all your works may fear You and all crea-
> tures bow before You, that they may all form one band
> to perform your will with perfect heart. For we know,
> Lord our God, that dominion is yours, strength is in your
> hand and might in your right hand, that your name is
> awesome upon all whom You have created . . . Then
> shall the just see and be glad, the upright exult and the
> pious sing for joy. Iniquity shall close its mouth and all

wickedness shall be wholly consumed like smoke, when You make the dominion of arrogance to pass away from the earth.

The most famous of the liturgical poems on these holy days is the *unetaneh tokef:*

We celebrate the mighty holiness of this day, for it is one of awe and dread. Thereon is your dominion exalted and your throne established in mercy, and You sit thereon in truth. Truly it is You alone who are judge and arbiter, who knows and witnesses. You write down and set the seal, You record and number, You remember the things forgotten. You open the records and the deeds therein inscribed proclaim themselves, for the seal of every man's hand is set thereto. The great trumpet is sounded, the still, small voice is heard; the angels are dismayed, and fear and trembling seize hold of them as they proclaim, Behold the Day of Judgment. The very host of heaven is to be arraigned in judgment, for in your eyes they are not pure. All who enter the world You cause to pass before You like a flock of sheep. As a shepherd seeks out his flock and causes it to pass beneath his crook, so do You cause to pass and number, tell and visit, every living soul, appointing the measure of every creature's life and decreeing its destiny.

On the first day of the year it is inscribed and on the Day of Atonement it is sealed, how many shall pass away and how many shall be born, who shall live and who shall die, who at the limit of a man's days and who before it, who shall perish by fire and who by water, who by the sword and who by wild beasts, who by hunger and who by thirst, who by earthquake and who by plague, who by strangling and who by stoning, who shall have rest and who shall go wandering, who shall be tranquil and who shall be harassed, who shall be at ease and who shall be afflicted, who shall become poor and who shall wax rich, who shall be brought low and who shall be upraised. But penitence and prayer and charity avert the evil decree.

For according to your name so is your praise. You are slow to anger and ever ready to be reconciled, for You desire not the death of the sinner but that he turn from his way and live. Even until the day of his death You wait for him, and if he return You straightway receive him. In truth You are their Creator who knows their nature, that they are flesh and blood. As for man, he is from the dust and unto the dust shall he return. He gets his bread with the peril of his life. He is like a fragile potsherd, like the grass that withers, like the flower that fades, like a fleeting shadow, like a passing cloud, like the wind that blows, like the floating dust, like a dream that flies away. But You are King, God living and everlasting.

The night of Yom Kippur is the only time when men put on the *tallit* for an evening service. (It is worn throughout the day on Yom Kippur except in Reform synagogues.) The Yom Kippur evening service begins with the recitation of the *kol nidrei*, a legal renunciation of vows that the worshipper has made to God but was unable to fulfill. According to halaka, one should not expect forgiveness from God unless his vows have been fulfilled. It is necessary, therefore, for one to formally renounce the vows that he was unable to keep before he can present his confession of sin to God and ask his forgiveness. The confession is made later on in the evening and is repeated at the other services during the day. It is not personal in nature, but is worded in the plural ("*we* have sinned, *we* have transgressed . . .") since the people pray for one another as well as for themselves. God is beseeched to inscribe and seal the entire people of Israel, not merely the individual seeking his own personal salvation, in his Book of Life. In synagogues that follow the Ashkenazic tradition, the *kol nidrei* is chanted to a hauntingly beautiful melody that dates from about 1500. People feel that the music of *kol nidrei* is the most magnificent in the entire

Jewish liturgical tradition, and many come to the synagogue specifically to hear it.

The concluding service on Yom Kippur day is also most impressive. Its prayers beseech God to keep the gates of mercy and repentance open, even as the gates of heaven close with the setting of the sun.

> Open for us the gate, at the time of the closing of the gate, for the day is turned. The day turns, the sun sets and turns, we would come into your gates. . . . God, King, who sits upon a throne of mercy, who governs Himself with kindness, forgiving his people's sins and causing them to pass away one by one, abundant in pardon to sinners and forgiveness to transgressors, acting charitably with all who are made of flesh and spirit, not in accordance with their evil do You recompense them. God, You have taught us to repeat the Thirteen Attributes (Exodus 34:6–7). Remember unto us this day the covenant of the Thirteen Attributes as You did make it known to the Meek One (Moses) in days of old, as it is written, The Lord descended in a cloud and stood with him there and proclaimed the name of the Lord. The Lord passed by before him and proclaimed, "The Lord, the Lord, God, merciful and compassionate, long suffering and abundant in kindness and truth, doing kindness unto thousands, forgiving iniquity, transgression and sin, and acquiting." So forgive our iniquities and our sins and take us as your inheritance.

Before the *shofar* is sounded to end the service, the congregation repeats once, "Hear, Israel, the Lord is our God, the Lord is One." Then three times, "Blessed be the name of his glorious kingdom forever and ever." And then seven times, "The Lord. He is God."

It is important to note that repentance on the Day of Atonement brings forgiveness only for sins against God. Sins committed against a fellow man or woman can be forgiven only if one first makes an attempt to appease the person who was wronged. (Mishna Yoma 8:9)

Sukkot

The festival of Sukkot (Tabernacles) commences on the fifteenth of Tishri and lasts for seven days. In Israel and among Reform and Reconstructionist Jews the first day is a full holy day on which work should not be done. Orthodox and Conservative Judaism define the first two days as full holy days, since they follow the halakic ruling that when the Torah commands a one-day festival, Jews living outside the land of Israel should observe it for two days, the second day being the "second day holiday of the exiles." (This does not apply to Yom Kippur because it is a fast day.) The remainder of the week is a semiholiday during which normal work may be performed.

Sukkot is a feast of thanksgiving for the harvest and derives its name from the *sukka* ("booth" or "tabernacle") that observant Jews built to "dwell" in (or at least to eat in) during the festival week. The *sukka* is a temporary shelter with a roof of branches, twigs, and leaves through which the sky is visible. It may be attached to a family's house, or several families may jointly put one up. Most synagogues also have a *sukka* to which those in attendance repair after services for the blessing of the wine and the bread, followed by some light refreshment. A *sukka* is often decorated with fruit and flowers by children in a family or by the children in a synagogue's religious school. In Hasidic families and among others who follow the mystical tradition, there are "guests" who join the celebrants in the *sukka* for the blessings and the meals on each day of the festival. These "guests," in the order of their arrival, are Abraham, Isaac, Jacob, Moses, Aaron, Joseph, and David. The origin of the *sukka* is the booth that farmers in ancient times would build in the fields during the harvest. The Torah connects it to the temporary shelters of the Israelites during their journey in the desert following the Exodus from Egypt.

Besides the *sukka*, the other characteristic rite of the festival is the blessing of the *lulab*. This is a palm branch, together with a citron (*etrog*, a fruit of the citrus family), a branch of willow, and a sprig of myrtle, that the worshipper holds in his hands and waves in various directions on each day of the holiday (except on the Sabbath). Since the rainy season begins in Israel at the end of the Sukkot holiday, this rite no doubt originated in connection with it. In tradition, the rite is associated with the acknowledgment of God's sovereignty over nature.

At the services in the synagogue, a group of psalms known as *hallel* ("praise") is recited on each day of the holiday. On the full holy days, the full *hallel* is recited (Psalms 113–118), but on the days of semiholiday only a "half-*hallel*" is added. On each day of the holiday the worshippers make a joyous circuit about the sanctuary with *lulab* and *etrog* in hand; on the seventh day this processional is performed seven times.

On the day after Sukkot, the festival of *Shemini Aseret* ("the Eighth Day of Conclusion") is celebrated. Orthodox and Conservative Jews add another day called *Simhat Torah* ("the Rejoicing of the Torah"). In Israel and among Reform Jews only the first day is observed. The *sukka* and *lulab* have been set aside, but these concluding days continue the theme of joyful thanksgiving that characterized the festival week. On this last festival day, the final verses of Deuteronomy are read from the Torah scroll in the synagogue, and immediately thereafter the first verses of Genesis are read. This symbolizes the never-ending attachment of the people to the Torah, that no sooner is the reading of the sacred book completed than it is immediately begun again. On this day, all of the scrolls are taken from the Ark and paraded around the synagogue, the people joining in procession behind them and, in some cases, dancing with the scrolls. It is a particularly exciting time for children and constitutes a fitting conclusion to the cycle of holy days that began with Rosh haShana.

Pesah and Shabuot

The great spring festival of Judaism is _Pesah_ (Passover), beginning on the fifteenth of Nisan. It is so called because the angel of death "passed over" the houses of the Israelites when he struck down the first-born of Egypt, the last plague visited upon the Egyptians just prior to the Exodus. The festival begins on the day of the full moon following the spring equinox (or, in the case of a leap year, the full moon about one month later). In Israel and among Reform and Reconstructionist Jews the celebration lasts for seven days. The first day and the seventh day are full holidays on which work should not be performed. Orthodox and Conservative Jews outside of Israel observe the first two days as well as the seventh day and an added eighth day as full holidays. The remaining days of the festival week are semi-holidays on which work may be done.

The great event of the Passover is the Seder meal (_seder_ means "order") that takes place on the first night (or the first two nights) of the festival. This is the commemoration of the Exodus from Egypt and the birth of Israel as a free people, subject only to God. The meal begins with the _kiddush_ over the wine, but three additional cups must be consumed before the celebration is over, in thanksgiving for the four promises of redemption from bondage in the book of Exodus: "I will bring you out from under the burdens of Egypt; I will save you from their service; I will redeem you with an outstretched arm; I will take you as my people." The paschal lamb is no longer sacrificed as it was in biblical times, but there is a roasted bone on the table as a reminder. The _matsa_ (unleavened bread) is still present, as is the _maror_ (bitter herb), a reminder of the bitterness of slavery. These are blessed and eaten before the rest of the meal is served. Also in advance of the meal is the reading of the _haggada_ ("narration"), the retelling of the story of bondage and deliverance in response to the questions asked by the youngest person at the table ("Why is this night differ-

ent from all other nights? . . ."). An overriding theme in
the *haggada* is that

> in every generation each person is obliged to see himself
> as if he had himself come forth from Egypt. . . . There-
> fore we are obliged to rejoice before Him who did these
> wonders for us and for our ancestors. He brought us
> from slavery to freedom, from sorrow to joy, from mourn-
> ing to festivity, from darkness to great light, from servi-
> tude to redemption.

After the meal the concluding grace is recited, followed
by several songs. The Seder is a time when very many Jews
seek to join with their extended families, often traveling
long distances to be able to do this.

On the remaining days of the holiday only unleavened
products may be eaten, and observant Jews will not eat
anything that has not been properly supervised during its
preparation lest it have become contaminated by leaven. On
the day before the holiday, Orthodox Jews search their
houses for any crumbs of leaven and then burn what they
find. Houses are thoroughly cleaned in advance of Passover,
and dishes that are kept in reserve only for Passover are
used during the entire time of the festival. At the synagogue
services the Scripture lessons relate the story of the Exodus.
The full set of *hallel* psalms is recited on the first two days of
the holiday, but only the "half-*hallel*" on the other days, a
sign of sorrow that the Egyptians had to drown while Israel
crossed the Red Sea. According to tradition, the crossing of
the sea took place the seventh day.

The night that falls at the conclusion of Passover is a time
of special celebration among Moroccan Jews. This is the
Maimuna festival (from the Arabic for "wealth and good
fortune"). Moroccan Jews are numerous in France and French
Canada, and especially in Israel (other Israelis have adopted
the Maimuna from their Moroccan neighbors). People don
festive clothes to visit their friends, relatives, and neighbors.
Each household sets up a table holding dishes of honey,

sweets, fruits, nuts, dates, yeast cakes (which were forbidden, of course, during the Passover week), pancakes, wine, and milk, from which the visitors partake. It is a time for exchanging best wishes for prosperity and success during the year ahead.

Beginning with the second day of Passover, traditional Jews, in response to biblical commandment, ritualistically "count" the seven full weeks that follow. Each night they number the day, reciting the appropriate blessing for the act of counting. Orthodox and Conservative Jews are not supposed to get married during this period of "counting," nor should they cut their hair. (Certain days within this period, however, are exempt from these prohibitions.) The traditional explanation for these gestures of mourning is that at this season during the second century A.D. a great plague had struck down many pupils of the sages. In actuality, however, these prohibitions reflect similar practices in many other societies, where the days or weeks preceding the harvest and the beginning of the agricultural year constitute a period during which it is considered bad luck to marry or rejoice too greatly. At the conclusion of the seven weeks, on the sixth of Sivan, the festival of *Shabuot* ("Weeks" or "Pentecost") is celebrated (one day in Israel and by Reform and Reconstructionist Jews, two days by Orthodox and Conservative Jews). This is an ancient harvest festival, but it is also associated with the giving of the Ten Commandments. In Reform Judaism Shabuot is very often the day of Confirmation for young people in the synagogue religious school.

Hanukka and Purim

There are no other Jewish holidays that require a cessation from work; only occasions stipulated in the Torah include this obligation of "rest" as a facet of their observance. One of the festivals on which normal work may be performed is *Hanukka* (Dedication), falling at the season of the winter solstice. Hanukka begins on the twenty-fifth of Kislev and continues for eight days. While certain prayers and Scripture lessons are added to the daily worship services, including the *hallel* psalms, the characteristic observance of the holiday is the kindling of lights on each of its eight nights. Many Jews who are not particular about other rituals are quite likely to be very concerned to light the Hanukka lamp each night with the appropriate blessings—one candle on the first night (along with the "server" candle, the one used to light the others), culminating in eight on the last night.

Hanukka commemorates the victory of the Maccabean warriors against the forces of the Seleucid king in 165 B.C. and the subsequent rededication of the Temple to the worship of God. In talmudic tradition, the reason for the festival's being eight days long is attributed to the miracle of a small cruse of oil's burning for eight days in the Temple. The actual reason for the length of the festival, however, is that the Maccabees wished their rededication of the Temple to imitate the example of the dedication of Solomon's Temple, which occurred during the Feast of Tabernacles and which is eight days long. Jews today are very attached to the celebration of Hanukka because it calls to mind the heroism and courage of those who fought for religious freedom. The miracle that is celebrated, either in place of or in addition to a miracle involving a cruse of oil, is that of the victory of the few over the many, of those who fought to preserve their own way of life over imperial forces that tried with great cruelty to wrest away a people's traditions. Hanukka celebrations are usually centered in the home and include games and songs for children. In recent years it has become a major occasion for the exchange of gifts, responding to the influence of the Christmas season, which is also a festival of the winter solstice.

Another widely celebrated Jewish holiday is *Purim* (Lots), on the fourteenth of Adar. This commemorates the victory of the Jews of Persia over Haman, the wicked adviser to the king who sought to destroy the Jews, as related in the book of Esther. This is the Jewish carnival time, when otherwise very sober people will dress in costume and mimic authority, and perhaps even consume a bit too much alcohol for proper dignity. All of this is not only allowed but is even encouraged on Purim. The major ritual observance of Purim is the reading of the *megilla*, the scroll of Esther, that tells of Haman's casting lots (*purim*) to select an auspicious time when he might send his forces against the Jews of the empire. The lot fell on the month of Adar, and the day selected for the murder and plundering of the Jews was the thirteenth. (For this reason Orthodox Jews fast from sunrise to sunset on that day.) Through the efforts of Esther, the Jewish queen of the empire, and her cousin Mordecai, Haman's plans were frustrated and the Jews were able to defeat and destroy their enemies on the very day that had been selected for their own destruction. The next day, the fourteenth, was when the Jews celebrated their victory.

The book of Esther is written as a humorous story with many farcical touches. It was perhaps not meant by its author to be taken as accurate history, but Jews through the ages have been inspired by it to recall that sometimes, when destruction seems most imminent, salvation may very well come in its stead. When the *megilla* is read in the synagogue, it is the custom for much noise to be made when Haman's name is mentioned. It is permissible to use metal or wooden noisemakers or stamp one's feet on the floor, all in the spirit of uninhibited fun. Purim, quite naturally, is very much enjoyed by children and is an occasion when people give gifts to their neighbors and to the poor.

Yom haShoa and Yom haAsma'ut

One of the newer observances that has been introduced into the Jewish calendar in some congregations and communities is that of *Yom haShoa* (Holocaust Memorial Day). This falls on the twenty-seventh of Nisan and memorializes the heroism of the fighters in the Warsaw Ghetto who rose in revolt against the Nazis in 1943, as well as all those others slain in the Holocaust of the Jews during World War II. Some American Jewish groups commemorate the day with memorial services during the nearest weekend, but others arrange gatherings on the day itself. In Israel the day is widely observed by all Jews, and places of entertainment and businesses are closed. It is a somber day devoted to speeches and elegies of remembrance. A common theme in many of the presentations is that "never again" will Jews allow such an event as the Holocaust to occur.

Another recent addition to the calendar is the celebration of *Yom haAsma'ut* (Israel's Independence Day) on the fifth of Iyyar. Coming just a few days after the Holocaust Memorial, this day, marking the emergence of the new State of Israel in 1948, offers its counterpoint of redemption to the theme of destruction emphasized in the earlier observance. In Israel, of course, Yom haAsma'ut is a major occasion. The eve of the holiday is observed as a memorial to those who died in the War of Independence, so places of entertainment are closed and the usual noise and bustle of Israeli life is reduced to a minimum. But when the holiday itself begins, the mood changes completely. There are parades, dances, and celebrations of all kinds. Many of the synagogues in Israel add the *hallel* psalms of praise to their services, although some of the more rigid Orthodox do not.

In America, and elsewhere in the Jewish world, Yom haAsma'ut is observed by some Jews but not, at least as yet, by the majority. It is the policy of some synagogues, including Reform, Conservative, Reconstructionist, and "modern Orthodox," to include the *hallel* psalms in services for the day, but others in these groups do not. Some community groups and synagogues choose to commemorate Israel's independence with celebrations on a weekend rather than on the day itself.

Tisha b'Ab

In Orthodox Judaism there are four fast days connected with the siege and destruction of Jerusalem by Babylon in 586 B.C. These occur on the third of Tishri, the tenth of Tebet, the seventeenth of Tammuz, and the ninth of Ab. The first three of these fasts extend only from sunrise to sunset. The fast of the ninth of Ab (*Tisha b'Ab*) is very different, however. This is the day when the Babylonians destroyed the Temple, and it is also the day when the Romans destroyed the second temple in 70 A.D. It is, accordingly, a day of great importance in Orthodox and Conservative Judaism. (Some Reform Jews observe the day as well, although the majority do not.) In Orthodox and Conservative practice no marriages may be performed during the three weeks leading up to Tisha b'Ab, nor should Jews listen to music or take haircuts or shaves. During the nine days prior to Tisha b'Ab, one should not eat meat or drink wine except on the Sabbath, although the sick who may need these things for therapeutic purposes are exempted from the prohibition. Bathing is forbidden during these nine days as well, except for the sick or in preparation for the Sabbath. (These restrictions are not observed by Reform Jews.) The fast of Tisha b'Ab is as rigorous as that for Yom Kippur, lasting from sunset to sunset.

On the evening of Tisha b'Ab the worshippers who gather at the synagogue remove their shoes and sit on the floor in near darkness. Besides the evening service, the biblical book of Lamentations is chanted in a mournful mode. The service the next morning is the only one during the year when the worshippers do not wear *tallit* and *tefillin*. These are adornments of splendor, hence not fitting to be worn at this time that commemorates deepest tragedy. At the afternoon service, however, which takes place toward the end of the tragic day, the worshippers do don *tallit* and *tefillin*, for tragedy and destruction will give way to redemption and favor. The theme of redemption is carried through on the Sabbath that immediately follows Tisha b'Ab, for the lesson from the Prophets that day is: "Comfort, comfort my people, says your God. Speak tenderly to Jerusalem and cry out to her that her time of service is ended, that her iniquity is pardoned, for she has received from the Lord's hand double for all her sins." (Isaiah 40). Similar messages of comfort are read from the books of the Prophets on all the seven Sabbaths that fall between Tisha b'Ab and Rosh haShana. An old belief is that the Messiah will be born on Tisha b'Ab.

CHAPTER TEN

The Messiah and the World-to-Come

The speculations about a Messiah ("anointed one"), a king who would be God's chosen ruler over the Jews and the entire world, are rooted in interpretations of various verses in the books of the Prophets that were meant originally to apply to the kings of ancient Judah. During the time of the Hasmonean monarchy, however, and thereafter in the days of Herod and the Roman governors of Judea, the hope grew among many Jews that a righteous ruler would come to replace the wicked and rapacious ones who held sway over the people, and these verses were taken as predictions of a new king from the house of David, whom God would send. The Jerusalem Targum to Genesis 49:10–12 yields a dramatic picture of what the popular expectation was:

> The kingdom belongs to King Messiah and unto him are all the kings of the earth destined to render service. How beautiful is King Messiah, who will arise out of the house of Judah. He girds his loins and goes forth to war against his enemies, slaying kings and rulers. The rivers are red with the blood of the slain and the hills are white with the fat of warriors. His garments drip with blood and he himself is like one who treads the grapes. But how beautiful are the eyes of King Messiah, more beautiful than

pure wine, for they refuse to look upon sexual impurity
or the shedding of innocent blood. His teeth are whiter
than milk, for they do not eat the fruit of violence and
robbery. The mountains become red with vines, the vats
with wine. The hills become white with grain and with
flocks of sheep.

The messianic king, then, would be a mighty warrior in
battle against his enemies, but thereafter he would reign
over his people in righteousness and, as a consequence, the
earth would yield its increase. Later Jewish conceptions of
the Messiah picture him as a teacher and interpreter of
Torah as well.

During the first or second century A.D. in addition to the
hope for a victorious Messiah of the house of David, a belief
arose that there was to be yet another Messiah, a descendant of one of the lost tribes of Israel, specifically Joseph,
who would die in battle against the hordes of the wicked
who would war against God and his people at the gates of
Jerusalem. This Messiah, along with all the righteous, would
be restored to life at the resurrection of the dead that would
take place after the final victory of Israel over the enemies
of God.

In Jewish speculation, the prophet Elijah, who, according
to the book of Kings, rose to heaven without tasting death,
will return as the prophet of the end of days to announce
the appearance of the Messiah son of David. The Jews will
return from the four corners of the earth to the land of
Israel, and the Temple will be rebuilt. Elijah will answer all
the unsolved question of halaka with which the reconsti-
tuted nation will have to deal, and he will define who is a
genuine *kohen* eligible to serve as a priest in the new Temple.

The discovery of the Dead Sea Scrolls has revealed the
messianic concept of the Essene sect. The Essenes appear to
have expected the coming of a Prophet "like Moses" and
the "Messiahs of Aaron and Israel"; that is, a royal figure of
the line of David and a priestly figure who would be the
supreme ruler. This concept of the three Messiahs helps

modern scholars understand the beginnings of Christianity. Jesus was believed by his followers to have fulfilled all three roles. During his life he was the Prophet; through his death he served as the King (since some of the Essenes seem to have believed that the King would have to die); and as a result of his resurrection and expected return, he would be the Priest (since the heavenly Priest was expected to come down to earth as the ruler of the new age). The three figures also appear in a classic Jewish text, the Jerusalem Targum to Exodus 12:42:

> When the world comes to its fulfillment and is redeemed, the bands of wickedness will be smashed and the yokes of iron destroyed. Moses will emerge from the desert and King Messiah from Rome. . . . The Word of the Lord will lead them both, and they will come forth together as one. This is the Passover night of the Lord, guarded and reserved for all the generations of Israel.

There were, of course, many fanciful and miraculous expectations that grew up in conjunction with the belief in a Messiah. Many of these conceptions were ridiculed by the more rationalistic Jewish philosophers, and Maimonides' view of the messianic phenomenon in his twelfth-century commentary to chapter 10 of Mishna Sanhedrin became quite widely accepted among Orthodox Jews and others who retain the messianic hope. (Reform Jews and most other non-Orthodox interpret the Messiah not in a personal sense, but rather as the symbol of a purified and better world.) Maimonides wrote that there were several groups of misinformed people. One group believes that, in the messianic age, men will be like angels: immortal, of great stature, and very prolific; this group believes also that the earth will produce ready-to-wear garments and baked bread. Another group believes that the resurrection of the dead will occur with the coming of the Messiah and that all the righteous will enjoy earthly blessings and never die again. A third group believes that after the Messiah has come and revived the dead, all will be translated to Paradise, where throughout eternity they will eat and drink and enjoy perfect health. Maimonides made clear he had little respect for views like these and the materialistic concerns that underlie them. He said that people of intelligence ought to know better than to subscribe to childish ideas of this type. In his view, the messianic age will be a time when Israel will regain its sovereignty and return to its land under the Messiah. He will be a great king, whose name will be known throughout the earth. All the nations that become subject to him will live in peace with him. There will, however, be no change in the course of nature. Although it will be easier for people to earn a livelihood, there will still be rich and poor, strong and weak. The greatest blessing of those days, he says, will be that humanity will be freed from the scourge of war and able to devote itself full-time to the study of philosophy and the fulfillment of God's laws. According to Maimonides, the Messiah will eventually die, and his son will follow him on the throne of Israel. There will be no immortality, but people will live much longer because they will not be afflicted by the troubles that are so numerous now. "We hope for the Messiah not because we will enjoy great prosperity, ride on horses, drink wine, and enjoy fine music, but because, under the rule of a righteous king and in the company of all the righteous, we will be able to benefit from his wisdom and closeness to God."

Even though the religious tradition from the time of the Talmud onward prohibited attempts to calculate the date of the Messiah's coming, this did not prevent claimants to the messianic title from arising in various periods and in various places. Since one of the traditions was that the coming of the Messiah would be preceded by many "travails" and persecutions, "messiahs" could be counted upon to proclaim themselves when such conditions prevailed. Messianic agitation was also spurred by mystical studies, particularly the Lurianic *kabbala*, which taught that the process of *tikkun* (the properly ordered arrangement of the worlds) was almost complete and that with correct mystical intensity the

Jewish people could cause the final redemption to come to pass.

The most widespread messianic movement in all of Jewish history took place during the middle of the seventeenth century. This centered about the person of Sabbetai Sebi, a kabbalist from Smyrna in Turkey. Jews in all parts of Europe and the Near East accepted his messianic claims and awaited his word to proceed to the Holy Land. Those who denied his messianic status often had to keep their doubts to themselves for fear of offending his followers, so devoted were they to his cause. It was only after Sabbetai became a Muslim, having been presented the choice of Islam or death by the Turkish authorities, that the movement collapsed; even then there remained secret "Sabbatians" in many Jewish communities for many years.

With the coming of the modern era, two movements arose in Judaism that redefined the messianic hope in different ways. Reform Judaism eliminated the belief in a Messiah and maintained that the redemption of the Jews was to be accomplished not by the people's return to its ancient homeland, but by the integration of Jews as full and equal citizens in the lands in which they reside, culminating eventually in an age of peace and universal brotherhood when all peoples will be linked under God in bonds of genuine affection. Zionism taught that Jews could no longer wait for God to send a Messiah; the people must rely upon its own devices, as well as the goodwill of other nations, to reconstitute itself as a national entity in the land of Israel. The State of Israel is the culmination of the Zionist dream. To some Jews the State itself is essentially the fulfillment of the messianic hope. To others the State is but "the beginning of the redemption," and God will bring his Messiah at some future time to lead all the world's Jews to their ancient homeland where the Temple will be rebuilt. A few of the most rigidly Orthodox deplore the State of Israel as a desecration because it is not governed by Torah law and is in itself evidence of a lack of faith that God will in his own time send his chosen ruler to bring his people home. And to some Jews the State of Israel is a state like any other, possessing no more or no less spiritual significance than any other; to those who think along these lines, only when a state conducts its affairs in accordance with humanity's highest moral and ethical values can it be said to participate in the redemptive process.

The Jewish messianic hope has been described by some as a major factor in the development of certain secular movements in modern times. Socialism and Communism, for instance, owe their origin to Karl Marx, who was of German-Jewish parentage. Although Marx was baptized at age six and raised as a Protestant Christian, some speculate that his exposure to Jewish messianic yearnings contributed to his own desire to free the proletariat from the chains of oppression imposed by the capitalist system. Sigmund Freud, the founder of psychoanalysis, was raised as a Reform Jew and given a liberal Jewish education. It has been said that it was the Jewish messianic hope that motivated him to seek a way to free people from servitude to their own unconscious drives. Indeed, it may well be that the Jewish background of these men, as in the case of other thinkers as well, moved them to develop as they did and to affect modern culture and events in such profound ways.

Most schools of thought in contemporary Orthodoxy follow Maimonides and await the coming of a human Messiah, who will be endowed with superior, but purely human, qualities. They do not believe that the course of nature will be changed when he comes. Therefore, they make a distinction between "the days of the Messiah" and those of "the world-to-come." The phrase "world-to-come" is often used to mean the life of the soul after death: In Jewish thinking, the supreme reward of the righteous in this world-to-come is the opportunity to study the sacred texts without interruption. The phrase is also used to refer to the new world that will come into being after the bodily resurrection of the dead and the last judgment. Thus, after the "days of the Messiah" will have been completed, heaven and earth as we know it will come to an end. The "world-to-come" will include a new heaven and a new earth wherein the righteous, who will have been resurrected, will live forever in bliss. According to some, the punishment of the wicked will be that they will not share in the resurrection; according to others, they will be resurrected for eternal punishment. Orthodox Judaism retains the conviction that the righteous will be resurrected body and soul for final judgment and life in the world-to-come. This is one of the reasons why numerous Orthodox Jews wish to be buried in the Holy Land, particularly on the Mount of Olives to the east of Jerusalem. This is the place where, according to tradition, the resurrection will occur. Those who are buried elsewhere will have to move via underground tunnels to this spot before they will be raised.

It is only the rare non-Orthodox Jew who subscribes to a belief in bodily resurrection and a supernatural world-to-come as the consummation of history. For most Reform, Conservative, and Reconstructionist Jews it is the responsibility of people everywhere, Jews and others, to work to bring the blessings postulated for the world-to-come to fruition, insofar as possible, in this world. Most Jews believe it is humanity's responsibility to perfect this "world of chaos" into the Kingdom of God so that at last the prophet's word might be fulfilled: "Then will I turn to the peoples a pure language, that they may all call upon the name of the Lord, to serve Him with one consent." (Zephaniah 3:9)

Afterword: A Personal Note

What this book has tried to do is to project Jewish history, religious practice, and doctrine in such a way that both Jews and non-Jews can gain an understanding of the major emphases that underlie the faith, and how these emphases motivate those people to whom the faith is important. I have tried also to encapsule, as fully and fairly as possible, the differences that distinguish the different groups within Judaism from one another. In all of these efforts I have tried, insofar as possible, to keep my own personal predilections out of the picture. If the reader who has gone through the entire book is unable, at its conclusion, to know just where I stand, then my effort in this regard has been successful.

The note on which this book began was that the Jews, for much of their history, have been "a people that dwells alone." Many Orthodox Jews, as well as a number of the non-Orthodox, still regard this as an ideal of Jewish existence. The people and its faith, they say, must retain its distance as far as possible from the practices and teachings of other groups. Many "modern Orthodox" Jews, and the majority of the non-Orthodox, would not agree that the Jews should seek to be "a people that dwells alone." They are convinced that all humanity constitutes one human family and that, while others can learn much from the Jews, so too can Jews learn much from other people. This is the attitude to which I subscribe. I probably belong to the more radical segment of the Reform group, believing that it is humanity's destiny to form one community united by shared ethical standards that can be summarized in the two commandments, "You shall love your neighbor as yourself" (Leviticus 19:18) and "The stranger who sojourns with you shall be the equal of the native born among you and you shall love him as yourself" (Leviticus 19:33). I do not believe that any religion has a monopoly on true insight; each seeks, rather, to know God and the way of life that it is best for humanity to follow. It is only when we can appreciate each other and the unique gifts that each person, and each people, possesses that we are able to progress along this way.

Over the thousands of years of Jewish history there have been countless Jews who subscribed to this vision. In our own day there are millions who continue to do so. They wish to make the teaching of the prophets, and of the later sages who continued their work, into the heritage of the Jewish people and all humanity. These are people who work for justice wherever injustice is found, who seek to plant seeds of love where hatred flourishes. These are men and women who give of their substance, and in some cases even life itself, that the world might be a better place because for a time they lived within it.

The Jewish faith and tradition is not the work of any single prophet or sage. It comes out of the history and experience of the entire Jewish people. It is rooted in the sense of covenant that links the entire people to God. Because there were so many occasions in its history when the Jewish people plumbed the depths of despair, Judaism must teach its followers to choose life not only for themselves but for the entire human family. Because Jews have so often known hate, they must become partisans of love. Because Jews have striven to know God and his will, they must work to make the moral law the heritage of all people. Jews of all types share a glorious heritage and history, but the challenges that are offered by the future ought to elicit responses every bit as inspiring as those encountered in the past.

Since this book includes a number of citations from the sages, we conclude with the words of the doxology recited when the words of the sages are studied:

Upon Israel and upon the teachers, upon their pupils and those who in turn learn from them, upon all who occupy themselves with the Holy Teaching here or elsewhere, upon us and upon them may there come grace and love and mercy from the Lord of heaven and earth. So say we—Amen.

Further Readings

Chapter Two: Ancient Israel

J. Bright *A History of Israel*. Philadelphia: Westminster Press, 1972.

N. Gottwald. *The Tribes of Yahweh*. Maryknoll, N.Y.: Orbis Books, 1979.

M. Noth. *The History of Israel*. New York: Harper and Row, 1960.

H. Ringgren. *Israelite Religion*. Philadelphia: Fortess Press, 1966.

Chapter Three: The Hebrew Scriptures

R. E. Friedman. *Who Wrote the Bible?* New York: Harper and Row, 1988.

M. Greenberg. *Understanding Exodus*. New York: Behrman House, 1969.

A. J. Heschel, *The Prophets*. New York: Harper and Row, 1962.

R. H. Pfeiffer, *Introduction to the Old Testament*, New York, Harper and Row, 1948.

W. G. Plaut. *The Torah: A Modern Commentary*. New York: Union of American Hebrew Congregations, 1981.

N. Sarna. *Understanding Genesis.* New York: Schocken Books, 1970.

Chapter Four: The Development of Judaism

S. Dubnow. *History of the Jews in Russia and Poland.* Philadelphia: Jewish Publication Society, 1916–20.

A. Guttmann. *Rabbinic Judaism in the Making: The Halakhah from Ezra to Judah.* Detroit: Wayne State University Press, 1970.

A. Hertzberg. *The Zionist Idea.* Garden City, N.Y.: Doubleday, 1959.

I. Howe. *World of our Fathers: The Journey of the East European Jews to America and the Life They Found and Made.* New York: Harcourt Brace Jovanovich, 1976.

S. Lieberman. *Hellenism in Jewish Palestine.* New York: Ktav Publishing House, 1962.

D. Novak. *Jewish-Christian Dialogue: A Jewish Justification.* New York: Oxford University Press, 1989.

E. Rivkin. *A Hidden Revolution: The Pharisees' Search for the Kingdom Within.* Nashville, Tenn.: Abingdon Press, 1978.

C. Roth. *A History of the Jews: From Earliest Times Through the Six-Day War.* Schocken Books, 1970.

H. M. Sachar. *The Course of Modern Jewish History.* New York: Dell, 1977.

H. M. Sachar. *A History of Israel.* New York: Alfred A. Knopf, 1976.

E. Schuerer. *The History of the Jewish People in the Age of Jesus Christ (175* B.C.–A.D. *135)*, a new English edition revised and edited by Geza Vermes and Fergus Millar. Edinburgh: T. and T. Clark, 1973.

R. M. Seltzer. *Jewish People, Jewish Thought.* New York: Macmillan, 1980.

G. Vermes. *The Dead Sea Scrolls: Qumran in Perspective.* London: Collins, 1977.

G. Vermes. *Jesus the Jew: A Historian's Reading of the Gospels.* London: Collins, 1973.

H. J. Zimmels. *Ashkenazim and Sephardim: Their Relations, Differences, and Problems as Reflected in the Rabbinic Responsa.* London: Oxford University Press, 1958.

Chapter Five: Rabbinic Writings

A. Cohen. *Everyman's Talmud.* New York: Schocken Books, 1975.

S. Freehof. *The Responsa Literature.* Philadelphia: Jewish Publication Society, 1955.

C. G. Montefiore and H. Loewe. *A Rabbinic Anthology.* Philadelphia: Jewish Publication Society, 1960.

J. Neusner. *Invitation to Midrash.* San Francisco: Harper and Row, 1989.

J. Neusner. *Invitation to the Talmud.* San Francisco: Harper and Row, 1989.

The Siddur

Book of Prayer According to the Custom of the Spanish and Portuguese Jews, edited and translated by David de Sola Pool. New York: Union of Sephardic Congregations, 1947. (Orthodox–Sephardic)

Daily Prayer Book, translated and annotated with an introduction by Philip Birnbaum. New York: Herbrew Publishing, 1954. (Orthodox–Ashkenazic)

Gates of Prayer: The New Union Prayerbook. New York: Central Conference of American Rabbis, 1978. (Reform)

Siddur Sim Shalom: A Prayerbook for Shabbat, Festivals and Weekdays, edited by Jules Harlow. New York: Rabbinical Assembly and United Synagogue of America, 1985. (Conservative)

Kol Haneshamah. Wyncote, Pa.: Reconstructionist Press, 1989. (Reconstructionist)

Chapter Six: Philosophy and Mysticism

M. Buber. *I and Thou*. New York: Scribner, 1958.

J. Guttmann. *Philosophies of Judaism: The History of Jewish Philosophy from Biblical Times to Franz Rosenzweig*. New York: Holt, Rinehart and Winston, 1964.

A. J. Heschel. *God in Search of Man*. Philadelphia: Jewish Publication Society, 1956.

B. Holtz. *Back to the Sources*. New York: Summit Books, 1984.

I. Husik. *A History of Medieval Jewish Philosophy*. Philadelphia: Jewish Publication Society, 1958.

M. Mendelssohn. *Jerusalem and Other Jewish Writings*, translated by Alfred Jospe. New York: Schocken Books, 1969.

R. A. Rosenberg. *The Anatomy of God: The Book of Concealment, Great Holy Assembly and Lesser Holy Assembly of the Zohar*. New York: Ktav Publishing House, 1973.

F. Rosenzweig. *The Star of Redemption*, translated by William W. Hallo. New York: Holt, Rinehart and Winston, 1971.

G. Scholem. *Kabbalah*. New York: Quadrangle, 1974.

G. Scholem. *Major Trends in Jewish Mysticism*. New York: Schocken Books, 1954.

H. A. Wolfson. *Religious Philosophy: A Group of Essays*. New York: Atheneum, 1965.

Chapter Seven: Modern Judaism

Emet reEmunah: *Statement of Principles of Conservative Judaism*. New York: Jewish Theological Seminary of America, Rabbinical Assembly, United Synagogue of America, 1988.

M. Kaplan. *Judaism as a Civilization*. New York: Macmillan, 1934.

D. Philipson. *The Reform Movement in Judaism*. New York: Ktav Publishing House, 1967.

W. G. Plaut. *The Rise of Reform Judaism: A Sourcebook of Its European Origins*. New York: World Union for Progressive Judaism, 1963.

W. G. Plaut. *The Growth of Reform Judaism: American and European Sources Until 1948*. New York: World Union for Progressive Judiasm, 1965.

H. M. Rabinowicz. *Hasidism: The Movement and Its Masters*. Northvale, N.J.: Jason Aronson, 1988.

M. Sklare. *Conservative Judaism: An American Religious Movement*. New York: Schocken Books, 1972.

Chapter Eight: The Jewish Household

M. D. Bial. *Liberal Judaism at Home*. New York: Union of American Hebrew Congregations, 1971.

H. Donin. *To Be a Jew: A Guide to Jewish Observance in Contemporary Life*. New York: Basic Books, 1972.

S. J. Einstein and L. Kukoff. *Every Person's Guide to Judaism*. New York: Union of American Hebrew Congregations, 1989.

M. Steinberg. *Basic Judaism*. New York: Harcourt Brace Jovanovich, 1947.

Chapter Nine: The Calendar and the Holy Days

T. H. Gaster. *Festivals of the Jewish Year*. New York: William Sloane, 1953.

High Holy Day Prayerbooks

Prayers for the New Year and the Day of Atonement According to the Custom of the Spanish and Portuguese Jews, edited and translated by David de Sola Pool. New York: Union of Sephardic Congregations, 1948–1949. (Orthodox–Sephardic)

Service of the Synagogue: New Year and Atonement (The Adler Mahzor). New York: Hebrew Publishing, 1959. (Orthodox–Ashkenazic)

Gates of Repentance: The New Union Prayerbook for the Days of Awe. New York: Central Conference of American Rabbis, 1978. (Reform)

Mahzor for Rosh Hashanah and Yom Kippur, edited by Jules Harlow. New York: Rabbinical Assembly, 1972. (Conservative)

H. Schauss. *The Jewish Festivals.* New York: Union of American Hebrew Congregations, 1938.

Chapter Ten: The Messiah and the World-to-Come

J. H. Greenstone. *The Messiah Idea in Jewish History.* Philadelphia: Jewish Publication Society, 1948.

G. Scholem. *Sabbatai Sevi: The Mystical Messiah.* Princeton, N.J.: Princeton University Press, 1973.

Index

211

C

D

E

K

J

L

T

U